WRITERS AND THEIR WORK

ISOBEL ARMSTRONG
General Editor

SIR WALTER SCOTT

SIR WALTER SCOTT

From the portrait , *c*. 1824, by Sir Edwin Henry Landseer

SIR WALTER SCOTT

Harriet Harvey Wood

NORTHCOTE

BRITISH COUNCIL

ATLANTIC
PUBLISHERS & DISTRIBUTORS (P) LTD

This edition is published by

ATLANTIC

PUBLISHERS & DISTRIBUTORS (P) LTD

7/22, Ansari Road, Darya Ganj, New Delhi-110 002
Tel: 40775252, 23273880, 23275880, 23280451; Fax: +91-11-23285873
E-mail: orders@atlanticbooks.com; Web: www.atlanticbooks.com

By arrangement with
Northcote House Publishers Ltd
Horndon House, Horndon, Tavistock, Devon, PL19 9NQ,
United Kingdom. (T)+44(0)1822 810066; (F)+44(0)1822 810034
(E) northcote.house@virgin.net and (W) www.northcotehouse.co.uk
The *Writers and their Work* series is published in association with the British Council.

First Indian Reprint 2010
First published in 2006 by Northcote House Publishers Ltd

ISBN 978-81-269-1312-1

British Library Cataloguing-in-Publication Data
A catalogue record for this book is available from the British Library

Typeset by TW Typesetting, Plymouth, Devon
Printed in India at Nice Printing Press, A-33/3A, Site-IV,
Industrial Area, Sahibabad, Ghaziabad, U.P.

To Nigel Thomson

Another Sheriff Extraordinary

Contents

Biographical Outline

1771	Walter Scott born on 15 August in College Wynd, Edinburgh, to Walter Scott WS and his wife Anne Rutherford.
1773	Sent to grandfather's farm at Sandyknowe to recuperate from infantile paralysis.
1775	Death of grandfather; sent to Bath to drink the waters.
1778	Returns to father's new home at 25 George Square, Edinburgh.
1779	Sent to Royal High School in October.
1783	Entered at Edinburgh University.
1786	Apprenticed to father while still a student.
1787	Near-fatal haemorrhage; sent to Kelso to recuperate.
1792	Called to the bar.
1795–6	Scott's abortive love affair with Williamina Belsches.
1797	Marries Charlotte Carpenter, Christmas Eve. Instrumental in founding Edinburgh Volunteer Light Dragoons, in which he was quartermaster.
1799	Publishes translation of Goethe's *Goetz von Berlichingen*. Appointed Sheriff of Roxburgh, Berwick, and Selkirk.
1800	Persuades James Ballantyne to move printing house to Edinburgh.
1802–3	Publication of *The Minstrelsy of the Scottish Border*.
1803	Visits Oxford and London.
1805	Publishes *The Lay of the Last Minstrel*.
1806	Appointed Clerk of Session (unsalaried till 1812).
1808	Publishes *Marmion* and *Life and Works of John Dryden*; completes *Queenhoo Hall* for John Murray.

1809	Sets up John Ballantyne as independent publishing house; organizes takeover of Theatre Royal, Edinburgh; collaborates in founding *Quarterly Review*.
1810	Publishes *The Lady of the Lake*.
1811	Purchase of Abbotsford (moved there in 1812).
1813	Publishes *Rokeby*. Failure of John Ballantyne and Co. Scott forced to borrow from friends to make up obligations.
1814	Publishes *Waverley* and *Life and Works of Jonathan Swift*. Voyage round the north of Scotland from Leith to Glasgow.
1815	Publishes *The Lord of the Isles* and *Guy Mannering*. Meets Byron and Prince Regent on visit to London. Visit to field of Waterloo and Paris.
1816	Publishes *The Antiquary*, *The Black Dwarf*, and *Old Mortality*.
1817	Publishes *Harold the Dauntless* and *Rob Roy*.
1818	Discovery of Scottish Regalia in Edinburgh Castle at Scott's instigation. Publishes *The Heart of Midlothian*.
1819	Scott seriously ill. Publishes *The Bride of Lammermoor*, *A Legend of Montrose*, and *Ivanhoe*. Death of Scott's mother.
1820	Scott made a baronet. Marriage of his daughter Sophia to John Gibson Lockhart. Publishes *The Monastery* and *The Abbot*.
1821	Death of John Ballantyne. Publishes *Kenilworth* and *The Pirate*. Birth of grandson, John Hugh Lockhart ('Hugh Littlejohn').
1822	Publishes *Peveril of the Peak*, *Halidon Hill*, and *The Fortunes of Nigel*. Masterminds George IV's visit to Edinburgh.
1823	Publishes *Quentin Durward* and *St Ronan's Well*. Maria Edgeworth's visit to Abbotsford.
1824	Publishes *Redgauntlet*.
1825	Starts keeping *Journal*. Publishes *The Betrothed* and *The Talisman*. The Lockharts move to London. Bankruptcy of Hurst and Robinson and of Constable, and Scott's ruin.

1826 Publishes *Woodstock*. Death of Lady Scott. Publishes *The Letters of Malachi Malagrowther* on the Scottish currency. Visit to London and Paris.

1827 Publishes *The Life of Napoleon* and first two volumes of *Chronicles of the Canongate* ('The Highland Widow', 'The Two Drovers', and 'The Surgeon's Daughter'). Scott acknowledges himself to be the author of *Waverley*.

1828 Publishes *The Fair Maid of Perth* and first series of *Tales of a Grandfather*. Beginning of work on the Magnum Opus edition of the collected novels.

1829 Publishes second series of *Tales of a Grandfather* and *Anne of Geierstein*.

1830 Scott has two strokes (February and November). Publishes *Tales of a Grandfather* (3rd series) and *Letters on Demonology and Witchcraft*.

1831 Publishes *Tales of a Grandfather* (4th series). Working on *Count Robert of Paris*. Third stroke (April). Publishes *Castle Dangerous*. Scott sails to spend winter in Malta and Italy. Death of John Hugh Lockhart.

1832 Begins *The Siege of Malta*. Leaves Italy for home in May. Fourth stroke at Nijmegen. Dies at Abbotsford on 21 September and buried in Dryburgh Abbey.

References and Abbreviations

There are innumerable editions of Scott's work, particularly of the novels. For consistency, references in the text to novels are to the Magnum edition (1829–33), the first complete edition published for the most part under Scott's supervision and with his notes. References are to the chapter. References to the poems are all taken, for the sake of consistency, from J. G. Lockhart's 1833–4 edition of the complete poems, which includes *The Minstrelsy of the Scottish Borders*.

The following abbreviations are used for the novels:

A.	*The Antiquary*
BL	*The Bride of Lammermoor*
CC	*Chronicles of the Canongate*
GM	*Guy Mannering*
I.	*Ivanhoe*
OM	*Old Mortality*
R.	*Redgauntlet*
RR	*Rob Roy*
T.	*The Talisman*
W.	*Waverley*

Abbreviations for other works by Scott are as follows:

J.	*The Journal of Sir Walter Scott*, ed. W. E. K. Anderson (paperback edition, Canongate Classics, Edinburgh, 1998)
L.	*The Letters of Sir Walter Scott*, ed. Sir Herbert Grierson (12 vols.; London, 1932)
SH	*Scott on Himself*, ed. David Hewitt (Edinburgh: Scottish Academic Press, 1981)

1

Introduction

> What a life mine has been. Half educated, almost wholly neglected or left to myself – stuffing my head with most nonsensical trash and undervalued in society for a time by most of my companions – getting forward and held a bold and clever fellow, contrary to the opinion of all who thought me a mere dreamer – Broken-hearted for two years – My heart handsomely pieced again – but the crack will remain till my dying day – Rich and poor four or five times – Once at the verge of ruin yet opend new sources of wealth almost overflowing – now taken in my pitch of pride and nearly winged (unless the good news hold) because London chuses to be in an uproar and in the tumult of bulls and bears a poor inoffensive lion like myself is pushd to the wall – And what is to be the end of it? (*J.* 51, 18 Dec. 1825)

So Scott summarized his own life at his time of greatest trial; the quotation comes at the end of the diary entry for the day on which his financial ruin was finally confirmed. The entry begins '*Venit illa suprema dies.* My extremity is come' (*J.* 46). Setting aside the anguish of mind in which it was set down, it is as good a potted autobiography as any writer has produced. Ahead of him lay six years of gruelling toil, which would make him an old man before his time, and physical and mental disintegration, which were to kill him by the age of 62. His literary career did not begin seriously until his thirties when he was already well established in his legal career. In the remainder of his life he was to pour out a list of publications – poetry, fiction, scholarly editing, biography, and journalism – which few other writers of any age could equal and none surpass. He was also to write a new chapter in the history of British authorship and bookselling.

It is the fashion nowadays to sneer at Scott as a second-rate writer of historical novels, an escapist, popular in his day but no longer a matter of concern for students of serious literature. It is a superficial judgement, encouraged to some extent by Scott himself, who was only too prone to undervalue his own achievements, and who did provide a certain amount of ammunition in the series of second-rate novels and hack work that he churned out between 1826 and 1831 in his efforts to meet his financial liabilities. No service is done to Scott by attempting to put *Old Mortality* and *The Heart of Midlothian* on the same level as *Castle Dangerous* and *Count Robert of Paris* (of which he himself said, 'I think it is the public are mad for passing those two volumes. But I will not be the first to cry them down in the market' (*J.* 784, 28 Feb. 1832)). It is a sobering thought that if he had opted for bankruptcy in 1826 (as, he frankly admitted, he would have advised any client in similar circumstances to do), and ceased to write then, his literary reputation would probably stand very much higher today than it does. It has, moreover, to be remembered that well before the crash of 1826, indeed for much of his literary career, Scott was writing desperately to cover urgent and outstanding financial commitments. Leavis denied him a place in his great tradition, describing him as 'a great and very intelligent man' who, not having the creative writer's interest in literature, made no serious attempt to work out his own form and break away from the bad tradition of the eighteenth-century romance. Out of Scott, he says, a bad tradition came. Setting aside Leavis's opinion of the merits of the eighteenth-century novelists admired by Scott (notably Fielding and Richardson), his judgements were often less than fair, and he was certainly less than fair to Scott, never more so than in accusing him of failing to work out his own form. This is conspicuously what he in fact did. No more unfair criticism could have been made of Scott than to accuse him of not being a creative writer.

Many writers' reputations decay after their deaths. Scott, who during his career enjoyed a degree of fame that it is difficult to imagine any writer enjoying today, confidently expected his reputation to sink in future years and would not have been surprised at the extent to which it has done so. In his generation, wrote Carlyle, no particularly warm friend to him, 'there was no literary man with such a popularity in any country; there have only been a few with such, taking-in all generations and all countries'.[1] In 1886 he was still coming second in popularity after Dickens in a survey of schoolgirl readership, and as late as the end of the nineteenth century, hotels far from where he lived were being christened the Kenilworth and the Ivanhoe, though few who pass them today would know why. In Edinburgh and Tweedside he has marked the landscape as indelibly as Shakespeare (with whom in his prime he was frequently and not entirely absurdly compared) did that of Stratford. In the words of one critic, 'Scotland as it is seen to-day is largely the creation of Walter Scott.'[2] In his day, he was not only the most widely known and read author in the world, he was certainly the most influential. When the financial crash of 1826 came, in which so many were affected, his misfortunes overshadowed those of every other sufferer and were regarded as a national catastrophe. When he lay dying in Jermyn Street in 1832, on his return from his ill-fated voyage to the Mediterranean, it was as if royalty were dying, and bulletins were issued daily.

To some extent there has been a re-evaluation of Scott in the last fifty years, and Leavis's damning verdict is no longer generally accepted, if, indeed, it ever was. His rehabilitation started in 1932 with Sir Herbert Grierson's biography and edition of his letters, a Herculean task; these were followed in 1951 by three influential essays: Arnold Kettle's chapter on *The Heart of Midlothian* in his *Introduction to the English Novel*, S. Stewart Gordon's 'Waverley and the Unified Design' in *English Literary History* (vol. 18), and, most important of all, David Daiches's 'Scott's Achievement as a Novelist' in *Nineteenth Century Fiction* (reprinted in Daiches's *Literary Essays* (1966)). Then came in 1955 Georg Lukacs's study of Scott in Marxist historicist terms in his *The Historical Novel*, which not only reassessed the importance of the historical novel generally but placed Scott in the context of the European novelists who succeeded him, and by Donald Davie's *The Heyday of Sir Walter Scott* (1961), which, in a wide-ranging study, compares his achievements with those of his disciples, the Russian Pushkin, the Pole Mickiewicz, and the American Fenimore Cooper.

Since then there has been a steady stream of additions to studies of Scott, many of them inspired by the bicentenary of his birth in 1971, the most important of which were Edgar Johnson's exhaustive critical life (1970) and W. E. K. Anderson's edition in 1972 of Scott's *Journal,* which for the first time made this important work generally accessible in a complete and accurate form. And, not least important, there has been a stream of essays from younger scholars like Ian Duncan, introducing modern paperback editions of the novels. His standing as a novelist is no longer seriously disputed in critical circles. None the less, he is not much read, especially by the young.

It was very different in his own lifetime. There is no greater testimony to Scott's popularity and the bookselling revolution he and his main publisher Constable produced between them than a letter written in 1848 by Robert Cadell, Constable's partner and one-time son-in-law and Scott's last publisher, when Cadell was negotiating to sell the Scott copyrights (out of which he had, morally speaking, cheated the Scott family). He speaks of the 'never-ceasing demand' for Scott's work, listing the various publications – novels, poems, the life of Napoleon, etc. – and writes:

> the figures would appear almost incredible and from the writings of one man – but so it is and during the progress of these doings I have paid Sir Walter Scott's debt and the debt on his estate of Abbotsford, in a word a trifle over £76,000 and what is more surprising as I have already said the demand for his work continues – aye, every hour, every minute of the day some one of them is called for, and a better proof I cannot give of this than that while I write to you I am told from home that twenty volumes of the novels, forty eight volumes of Prose twenty eight volumes [*sic*] must be reprinted forthwith to keep the market supplied.[3]

The equivalent value today of £76,000, itself only a fraction of what Scott's creativity and industry earned, would be in millions. The £10,000 (about £400,000 today) that Constable offered Scott for the biography of Napoleon would alone dwarf most literary advances paid in the twentieth century and Constable's confidence was justified by the £12,600 that Longman eventually paid for it. If this were his only claim to immortality, it would entitle him to an honourable place in the pantheon of booksellers, but little more. Novelists of indifferent ability have achieved colossal sales in our own days. But it is very far from being his only claim. His development of the historical novel and, even more, of the way in which his readers learned to apprehend history are serious literary claims to our continuing attention, as is his influence on the European novelists who followed him. More than any of these considerations, there are the novels: unequal in merit but (with the exception of the last two or three, written with a clouded brain under the influence of repeated strokes) consistent in their vitality and readability and almost always bearing the stamp of his creative genius. In the case of his greatest novels – *Waverley, Guy Mannering, The Antiquary, Old Mortality, Rob Roy, The Heart of Midlothian*, and *Redgauntlet* – his achievement was stupendous. Even the lesser novels are never less than gripping. He possessed the sublime, but nowadays often underrated, quality of readability.

2

Childhood and Youth

Before looking more closely at Scott's work, we should consider Scott's formation as a writer and, indeed, his ancestry and that half-educated childhood he spoke about in his journal. It is particularly necessary in Scott's case because of the exceptionally close and integral connection between his life and his work. The connection goes back to his ancestry, which deeply influenced his attitude to everything he did. 'Every Scotishman has a pedigree. It is a national prerogative as inalienable as his pride and his poverty,' he wrote in his memoirs (*SH* 2), and his perception of his own pedigree is inseparable from his poetry and novels. The Scotts were a large and widely spread border family, ranging in rank from the Duke of Buccleuch down to smallholders and sheep-farmers. The part of the Scott clan to which he belonged had been, in the not so distant past, border reivers, closely connected with the Scotts of Harden and the Scotts of Raeburn. His own financial problems were to stem mainly from his ambition to be the founder of the Scotts of Abbotsford, an innocent enough ambition in itself. Auld Wat of Harden (?1550–?1629), from whom he proudly claimed descent, had been an enthusiastic freebooter and sheep-stealer, and his own great-grandfather, another Walter Scott, was better known in Teviotdale by the nickname of 'Beardie', having taken a vow in 1688 never to shave until the Stuarts were restored to the throne. Beardie lost everything he had except his life in the Jacobite Rebellion of 1715, so that when his great-grandson was born in 1771, he found himself the grandson of a smallholder who raised sheep on land at Sandyknowe, near Smailholm (leased from more prosperous members of the Scotts of Harden), and the son of that sheep-farmer's eldest son, yet another Walter, who went to Edinburgh, became a Writer to the Signet (the most senior branch in Scotland of the profession of solicitor), and prospered. The spirit of Beardie was to coexist fruitfully in his great-grandson's veins throughout his life with the more sober whiggish inheritance of the lawyer.

But there were other strains in his ancestry that have to be taken into account in considering his literary career. His mother was the daughter of John Rutherford, Professor of Medicine in the University of Edinburgh, and of Ann, daughter of Sir John Swinton of Swinton, one of the oldest families in Scotland. On his mother's side, in fact, he was infinitely better connected socially than on his father's. But his mother brought other gifts into the family beside good blood and intelligence: it was from her that Scott derived his early love of poetry and reading. He seems to have been the only child in the family who inherited these characteristics to so marked an extent and this, combined with his childhood delicacy, built a particularly close relationship between them.

Scott was born healthy but suffered two severe illnesses in early life, the first an infection from a tubercular nurse in his early months, and the second an attack of infantile paralysis at eighteen months that nearly killed him and lamed him for life. He was sent to recover at his grandfather's farm at Sandyknowe, and stayed there till the age of eight, living mainly out of doors and cherished by grandparents and aunt. No more fortunate accident could have befallen a child of his temperament. The healthy open-air life he lived there, far removed from the smoke and drains of Edinburgh, the devoted attention of elderly relatives who had the leisure and the inclination (neither of which, it is probable, anyone in his own rather crowded home would have had) to read to him, and, above all, the solitude that encouraged him to read early for himself, all helped to develop his imagination. 'The love of Solitude was with me a passion of early youth when in my teens I used to fly from company to indulge visions and airy Castles of my own, the disposal of ideal wealth and the exercize of imaginary power,' he wrote many years later in his journal (*J.* 140, 28 Mar. 1826), but the passion was undoubtedly first developed in early childhood. At Sandyknowe, on his grandfather's instructions, he was carried up to the hills where the shepherd tended his sheep and laid down beside him, and, as he records,

> the natural impatience of a child soon inclined me to struggle with my infirmity and I began by degrees to stand, to walk, and to run although the limb affected was much shrunk and contracted. My general health which was of more importance was much strengthened by being frequently in the open air and, in a word, I who in a city had probably been condemned to hopeless and helpless decrepitude was now a healthy, high-spirited and, my lameness apart, a sturdy child. (*SH* 15)

His grandfather manufactured a crutch that enabled him to hobble about, but he was eventually able to discard it.

The death of his grandfather made little difference to his regime. His grandmother carried on the family farm, assisted by her brother-in-law, but found time to divert the invalid child with tales of border reivers whose exploits had in her own youth been a matter of recent tradition (and indeed, since one of the latest of them had married her aunt, of even closer interest than that). His aunt read and reread to him the few books that were to be found in the farmhouse: Ramsay's *Tea-Table Miscellany* and the ballad of *Hardyknute* were particular favourites, and he soon had much of them by heart. At the age of four, he was sent for a year to Bath to drink the waters, which did him little good, but where he was introduced to the theatre and Shakespeare; at the age of seven it was suggested that sea bathing would help the lame leg and he was taken to spend some weeks at Prestonpans, where he was introduced to an old friend of his father's, George Constable, who was many years later to be immortalized as the Antiquary. But from Prestonpans he was returned to his father's house in George Square, it being considered that he was now sufficiently robust to stand up to the rigours of Edinburgh and family life, and his formal education began.

The move cannot have been easy for him. He records himself that he felt 'the change from being a single indulged brat to becoming a member of a large family very severely' and admits that, spoiled by grandmother and aunt, he had 'acquired a degree of licence which could not be permitted in a large family', but adds: 'I had sense enough, however, to bend my temper to my new circumstances; but such was the agony which I internally experienced that I have guarded against nothing more in the education of my own family than against their acquiring habits of self-willed caprice and domination' (*SH* 19). Agony is a strong word, and Scott was not the man to use it lightly. His main consolation was reading poetry with his mother. His brothers did not share his literary tastes, and there is a strong suggestion that his and his mother's poetic pleasures were to be enjoyed in secret, not openly in the view of the strictly Calvinistic Walter Scott senior. In 1779 he was sent to the Royal High School.

In these early experiences, it is easy to see the sources of the characteristics that were to mark him in later life: the determination to struggle against the physical limitations that his lameness imposed on him; the love of solitude and of omnivorous reading; the pragmatic acceptance of and adjustment to difficulties; the self-control with which he learned to hide his fears and emotions even from those closest to him; most of all, the inclination to secrecy over the things that mattered most to him.

By his own account (probably exaggerated, since his claims agree ill with his boast that he was, according to the Rector of the High School, behind few in following and enjoying the meaning of Latin writers) he was a dull pupil at the High School, set, as he recorded later in a letter, 'to learn tasks to which I could annex neither idea nor utility' (*L.* ii. 262). If he was, as he claimed in his journal, indeed half-educated, it was not the fault of the High School, which offered a good education, and, from the time he went there, he was certainly not left to himself, except in so far as he followed the example of Dr Johnson and withdrew his attention to think about Tom Thumb. This he almost certainly did, his mind stuffed, if not with Tom Thumb, then with ballads, romances, fairy tales, travels, Shakespeare, and history. His memory for all these was formidable. Grierson claims in his biography that his reading of Vertot's *Knights of Malta* when he was confined to bed in 1784–5 could be reproduced virtually verbatim in his final work, *The Siege of Malta*, written during the last year of his life, although this story has been challenged by later critics.[1] His father supplemented the High School's curriculum with a private tutor, whose attentions Scott presumably shared with his brothers, and who instructed his pupils in writing, arithmetic, French, and the classics; typically, Scott derived the most profit from disputes with him on Church history: 'I hated presbyterians and admired Montrose with his victorious highlanders – He liked the presbyterian classes, the dark and politick Argyle . . . I took up my politics at that period as King Charles II did his religion, upon my idea that the Cavalier creed was the more gentlemanlike persuasion of the two' (*SH* 22).

Shortly after he had left the High School, however, his health let him down again, and in 1783 he returned to the border country to spend six months convalescing in Kelso with his aunt (his grandmother having by this time died), where his reading was random and undirected.

> A respectable subscription library, a circulating library of ancient standing and some private bookshelves were open to my random perusal and I waded into the stream like a blind man into a ford without the power of searching my way unless by groping for it. My appetite for books was as ample and indiscriminating as it was indefatigable and I since have had too frequently reason to repent that few ever read so much and to so little purpose. (*SH* 27)

During this period a number of things happened that were to have a greater or lesser influence on his future career. He fell in love for the first time, with the daughter of a Kelso shopkeeper; he encountered Percy's *Reliques of Ancient English Poetry*; and, most fateful of all, at the local Kelso school, which he attended spasmodically, he met James and John Ballantyne with whom his career was later to be so closely connected. Of these events, the first was by far the least important.

The full significance of his friendship with the Ballantyne brothers was not to become apparent for many years. Of more immediate importance was his discovery of Percy's *Reliques of Ancient English Poetry*. He described in his own memoir,

> with what delight I saw pieces of the same kind which had amused my childhood and still continued in secret the Delilahs of my imagination considered as the subject of sober research, grave

> commentary and apt illustration by an editor who shewed his poetical genius was capable of emulating the best qualities of what his pious labour preserved. I remember well the spot where I read these volumes for the first time. It was beneath a huge platanas tree in the ruins of what had been intended for an old fashioned arbour in the garden I have mentioned. The summer day sped onward so fast that notwithstanding the sharp appetite of thirteen I forgot the hour of dinner, was sought for with anxiety and was still found entranced in my intellectual banquet. To read and to remember was in this instance the same thing and henceforth I overwhelmed my schoolfellows and all who would hearken to me with tragical recitations from the ballads of Bishop Percy. (*SH* 28)

He had already discovered Macpherson's Ossianic forgeries and had initially been impressed by them, though, with a discernment that many of his older contemporaries lacked, he soon changed his mind. 'The tawdry repetitions of the Ossianic phraseology disgusted me rather sooner than might have been expected from my age' (*SH* 26). By the time he returned to Edinburgh to his classes at the university and to his clerking work in the chambers of his father, to whom he was apprenticed in 1786, he was well equipped for a future career as a Romantic poet.

It was not unusual in the 1780s (or indeed later) for a boy to go to university at the age of 12 or 13, since the early classes were more the equivalent of a sixth-form college than a university education.[2] Since he had enrolled as a student of humanities, his studies would have been mainly in Latin (in which he had done fairly well at school) and Greek, of which he apparently knew little, if anything. John Sutherland, in his biography, suggests that the elder Walter Scott pushed his son through his studies somewhat perfunctorily in order that he could be apprenticed to him at the normal age of 15 and settled to a safe career.[3] Scott speaks dutifully of his affection for his father and 'the rational pride and pleasure' he experienced in being useful to him, but he makes no secret of the fact that he heartily disliked the drudgery and confinement of the office, to which he was reconciled only by the money he could earn by transcribing legal documents. This was a strong incentive, and he recalls being able to write more than 120 folio pages without breaks for food or rest: certainly an invaluable training for the future novelist. It is possible that the strain of sitting so long over his desk may have been connected with another serious illness that he had in the second year of his apprenticeship, a haemorrhage from a broken blood vessel in his bowel. This was nearly fatal, and his convalescence was slow and difficult, and broke his university studies. He did not resume them until the winter of 1789.

Another advantage that the young Scott gained from employment in his father's chambers was acquaintance with his various Highland clients. The two Jacobite risings of 1715 and 1745, in favour of James VII of Scotland and II of England and his descendants of the exiled house of Stuart, had left much unfinished business behind them in the shape of fines and forfeited estates imposed on the defeated supporters of the Stuart cause, and this supplied a good deal of business for the Edinburgh lawyers. The elder Scott was no Jacobite himself, but numbered among his clients many who had been, like Alexander Stewart of Invernahyle, a veteran of both rebellions and a familiar figure to Scott from his boyhood. Invernahyle had the distinction of having fought with Rob Roy in earlier days, and from him Scott heard many of the stories of the Jacobite cause that were later to reappear in his novels. Through his legal affairs, and those of others like him, Scott was able in his apprentice days to make visits beyond the Highland line, where his reactions to the scenery and the squalor were not dissimilar to those of Edward Waverley and Frank Osbaldistone. It is rather unfair to accuse him of having romanticized the Highlands.

A particular pleasure of his university life was the company of a wider circle of friends than he had previously enjoyed. Scott has been criticized by biographers and others for his propensity for making friends in high places. The accusation is unjust. Throughout most of his life, he was more sought after by acquaintances of rank and influence than seeking. That he enjoyed such company is undeniable, nor is there anything remarkable in the fact that he should have done so. That he exploited the influence of such acquaintances when occasion arose is also undeniable; but this was the age of patronage, not the age of equal opportunities, and jobs were not open to application but were in the gift of the great. The Scott family was well connected, but the elder Scott was too unworldly a man to have access to much in the way of patronage himself. Scott himself was not immune from the occasional snobbish reaction, as when, in his teens, he spurned the offer of a fellow-student, Thomas Archibald, to help him with his deplorable Greek on the grounds that he was only the son of a tenant of one of his father's clients – a situation that his own grandfather had been in. Scott records the story himself, and, reading his version of it, one is tempted to wonder whether his reaction was due to snobbishness or to resentment of the criticism of his Greek. What is remarkable is not that Scott made use of the world as he found it, but that, despite the caresses and flatteries of the aristocracy that he enjoyed from early in his career, he managed to maintain a level head and discouraged his children from the kind of snobbery that, as he pointed out, made them ridiculous. At this stage, however, his companions were those whom he found around him at university, and, given the small, enclosed society of Edinburgh, it was inevitable that they came from widely varied social ranks; with them, and the help of the cash he earned in his father's office, he was able to enjoy an equally varied social life. As he said himself, it was not difficult for a youth with a real desire to please and be pleased to make his way into good society in Edinburgh.

During these early years of adulthood, therefore, he continued his studies, made many friends, indulged his antiquarian pursuits, and fell seriously in love for the first time with Williamina Belsches, daughter of Sir John Belsches and his wife, Lady Jane Stewart, of Fettercairn, Kincardineshire Scott felt himself to have received significant encouragement in his pursuit of her, but Williamina's parents had other views for their daughter than a penniless apprentice lawyer, and she was swiftly married to William Forbes, the heir to a baronetcy and to a bank. Scott was outclassed and distraught, but not for long; his own marriage to Charlotte Carpenter, a young Frenchwoman whom he met on holiday at Gilsland, took place within a year of Williamina's. In his own words, however, the crack in his heart made by Williamina never entirely healed; she is believed to have influenced the creation of Matilda in *Rokeby* and the mysterious Green Mantle in *Redgauntlet*.

In the meantime, the first professional decision that he was obliged to take was whether to join his father in partnership as a Writer to the Signet or whether to opt for the senior branch of the law and to become an advocate or barrister. In eighteenth-century Edinburgh the advocates were very much the *noblesse de la robe*, and enjoyed much greater social esteem than the writers. The bar, as he said himself, was 'the line of ambition and liberty' (*SH* 41); it could lead to the bench, to politics, and to much else besides. On the other hand, it could offer uncertain financial rewards, and Scott was aware that he was a poor public speaker. This would limit his chances of success and distinction there, but, for the qualified but briefless advocate, there were other possibilities if one had a little influence: there were, for example, sheriffdoms. He opted for the bar and eventually passed advocate in July 1792.

3

The Poetry

This is not the place to follow in detail Scott's professional and domestic career, a job that has been done by many biographers. It has been necessary to do so only in so far as it casts light on his subsequent development as a writer. Throughout his school and university years, his literary interests had been a strong undercurrent to his formal education, but there can never have been any idea in his head of becoming a professional poet or novelist. We find him, as he assumes the advocate's gown, in much the same condition as the young Waverley:

> he had read, and stored in a memory of uncommon tenacity, much curious, though ill-arranged and miscellaneous information. In English literature he was master of Shakespeare and Milton, of our earlier dramatic authors, of many picturesque and interesting passages from our old historical chronicles, and was particularly well acquainted with Spenser, Drayton, and other poets who have exercised themselves on romantic fiction, of all themes the most fascinating to a youthful imagination, before the passions have roused themselves and demand poetry of a more sentimental description. In this respect his acquaintance with Italian opened him yet a wider range. He had perused the numerous romantic poems which, from the days of Pulci, have been a favourite exercise of the wits of Italy, and had sought gratification in the numerous collections of *novelle*, which were brought forth by the genius of that elegant though luxurious nation, in emulation of the Decameron. In classical literature Waverley had made the usual progress, and read the usual authors; and the French had afforded him an almost exhaustless collection of memoirs, scarcely more faithful than romances, and of romances so well written as hardly to be distinguished from memoirs. The splendid pages of Froissart, with his heart-stirring and eye-dazzling descriptions of war and of

> tournaments, were among his chief favourites; and from those of Brantôme and De la Noue he learned to compare the wild and loose, yet superstitious character of the nobles of the League with the stern, rigid, and sometimes turbulent disposition of the Huguenot party. The Spanish had contributed to his stock of chivalrous and romantic lore. The earlier literature of the northern nations did not escape the study of one who read rather to awaken the imagination than to benefit the understanding. (*W.*, ch. III)

With this equipment, Scott embarked on his legal career, just at the moment when revolution and Romanticism were sweeping the world.

It was a period that might, without too much absurdity, be compared with the late-twentieth century. Revolutions in agriculture, industry, political and philosophical thought (like recent developments in technology) had changed the whole structure of society, bringing influxes of workers from the country to the town and altering the relationship between employer and employee. The tolerant liberalism of the Enlightenment was beginning to be replaced by the reactionary repression provoked by the French Revolution. Napoleon's conquests were bringing to birth new kinds of nationalism in, for example, Spain and Germany and a new kind of patriotism in Britain. At the time when Scott was entering on his new responsibilities, Wordsworth was in France, contemplating the excesses of the Terror, and Coleridge was planning a Pantisocratic community on the banks of the Susquehanna. Bishop Percy's *Reliques of Ancient English Poetry*, which had been so inspirational to Scott, had had wider effects on the Romantic movement as a whole. First published in 1765, this collection of old ballads, songs, and romances edited by Percy mainly from a seventeenth-century folio manuscript was immensely influential on the younger writers of the period and led to a complete reappraisal of the study of what Percy himself had apologetically described as 'the barbarous productions of unpolished ages'.[1] The book was to go through several editions by the end of the century, each containing new matter, and their effect on the rising literary generation was described by Wordsworth:

> I have already stated how much Germany is indebted to this work, and for our own country, its poetry has been absolutely redeemed

> by it. I do not think there is an able writer in verse of the present day who would not be proud to acknowledge his obligation to the *Reliques*. I know that it is so with my friends; and for myself, I am happy in this occasion to make a public avowal of my own.[2]

In addition to the inspiration provided by the *Reliques*, Scott had added the Ossianic forgeries to the catalogue of books read by Edward Waverley. He had, like so many of his contemporaries, discovered German literature, and had translated Burger, Schiller, and Goethe. His passive admiration of old ballads and legends, at first a secret passion, had developed into an active search for them. What was sanctioned by a bishop could not, after all, be regarded as unbecoming in a lawyer. Antiquarianism at this time was a respectable hobby (indeed, for many rich men, a respectable full-time occupation) and was closely allied to the interest in history that had been stimulated both by the work of Enlightenment philosophers like Hume and Robertson and by the constitutional questions that had been raised by the American and French revolutions. Scott has left it on record that the lectures that had impressed him most at university and that had had the most lasting effect on him had been those of Hume's nephew, another David Hume, who had taught Scots Law. The younger Hume derived eighteenth-century Scots law from its feudal origins, tracing its progress through the centuries, 'innovated, altered, broken in upon by the changes of times, of habits, and of manners, until it resembles some ancient castle, partly entire, partly ruinous, partly dilapidated, patched and altered during the succession of ages by a thousand additions and combinations' (*SH* 42). It would not be an exaggeration to say that these lectures were the most important single event in Scott's education. He was so affected by Hume's exposition that he copied out his notes of the lectures twice to impress them more effectively on his memory, and they certainly did as much to enlarge his ideas about historical development in general, in particular as it had affected Sçotland, as to confirm the antiquarian tastes that he was already indulging. Just as he was collecting oddments – a claymore and Lochaber axe given to him by Invernahyle, the saucer of the cup from which the traitor Murray of Broughton had drunk – so he embarked on his search for ballads, in which he enlisted many willing helpers. His first idea, proposed to his former Kelso friend, James Ballantyne, who by this time was a printer, was to publish a slim volume of what he described as riding ballads (those connected with the border raids) of the kind that had enchanted his childhood. What was eventually produced was the three-volume *Minstrelsy of the Scottish Border* (1802–3).

The publication has to be seen in the context of the collections of Scottish poetry and song that had started with Watson's *Choice Collection of Comic and Serious Scots Poems*, published in 1706 during the debate on the Union of Scotland and England as an assertion of Scottish identity, and continued through Ramsay's equally patriotically motivated *Tea-Table Miscellany* (which we know Scott had read as a boy) and *The Evergreen* to the various other eighteenth-century collections, which culminated in Burns's work. But it also shows throughout its compiler's debt to Percy's *Reliques*. In the first place, he accepted without question Percy's view of the origin of ballads, the idea of a minstrel as the original author of a ballad, though his composition might have been transmitted through and corrupted by oral tradition. The point is of interest in that it provided in due course the starting point for *The Lay of the Last Minstrel*, embodying Scott's conception of himself as the last minstrel of the Scott clan. In the second place he also accepted Percy's ideas of editorial responsibility – or lack of it. In his role as the latest of a line of minstrels, he collated different versions, he corrected and improved the rhythm and the rhyme, he interpolated stanzas of his own either where there were gaps in the original or where he felt he could improve on it. Many of the verses in the *Border Minstrelsy* that stick longest in the memory (for example, in 'The Twa Corbies') were probably never in any original text of the ballad, if indeed an original text existed at all. It has to be admitted that what he produced was more readable and exciting than a meticulous piece of scholarship would have been; the *Minstrelsy* points clearly forward to the future poet and novelist.

There has been considerable argument about the degree to which Scott 'improved' his sources, and it will probably never be possible to be certain how far he went. In the first place, Scott had as his enthusiastic ally in the preparation of the original edition his friend John Leyden, a poet and antiquarian as deeply steeped in the ballads of his native borders as Scott himself. Leyden, until his departure for the Far East in 1803 and his early death, undoubtedly had a hand in the texts and in any improvements that were made, and it would be impossible to distinguish his contributions from Scott's. The best discussion of the subject is a paper by Marryat Dobie, who has convincingly demonstrated that many of the apparent additions and emendations laid at Scott's door by later more critical editors like F. J. Child can be traced to written sources used by Scott and Leyden.[3] Apart from his famous folio manuscript, Percy had relied mainly on printed texts for the contents of the *Reliques*. Scott, on the other hand, looked primarily for oral sources, even if oral recitations were written down for his use. If one considers how many of his ballads relied on a variety of different sources provided by different reciters, it will be seen how impossible it would be to disentangle the process by which Scott's final texts reached the printed page. Even a single reciter will not necessarily produce a consistent text – as in the case of the Italian girl who sang a song several times, each time with a difference, and, when asked why, said she could not help it, *'mi viene così'*. Andrew Lang attributed to the more lasting oral tradition in Scotland the difference between the freshness and vitality of the Scottish versions and the relatively insipid and prosaic English ones. Scott's insistence on oral versions, where he could get them, may be sufficient to account for the greater readability of his texts, without assuming too much editorial intervention.

The difference between what Percy and Scott produced can best be illustrated from a famous ballad that both included: 'The Battle of Otterburn'. Percy prints his from a manuscript in the Cotton Library; it is in two parts and seventy stanzas, and it is pedestrian in the extreme. Scott's version is thirty-five stanzas, exactly half the length. Both are based on an episode, also recorded by Froissart, of a raid into Northumberland by the Scottish Earl of Douglas and his battle at Otterburn with Earl Percy of Northumberland, whom he had challenged to meet him there. During the battle, Douglas is killed. In the English version, the English are the winners; in the Scots version, the Scots win despite the death of their leader. It is difficult to compare them exactly, since the story told unfolds differently in each; what is not in question is the difference in the quality of the poetry and the dramatic force. Bishop Percy's version is full of the typical 'filler' clichés of ballad literature: 'withowtten drede', 'withowghten stryffe', 'fulle ryght', 'a man of strenghth'. It is a straightforward plodding account of the encounter. Scott's moves on to a completely different plane. When Douglas is warned that Earl Percy's army is approaching, the Bishop's version runs:

Awaken, Dowglas, cryed the knyght,
  For thow maiste waken wyth wynne:
Yender have I spyed the prowde Percy,
  And seven standardes wyth hym.

Nay by my trowth, the Douglas sayed,
  It ys but a fayned taylle:
He durste not loke on my bred banner,
  For all Ynglonde so haylle.

Was I not yesterdaye at the Newe Castell,
  That stonds so fayre on Tyne:
For all the men the Percy hade,
  He cowde not garre me ones to dyne.

He stepped owt at hys pavelyon dore
  To loke and it were lesse;
Arraye yow, lordyngs, one and all
  For here begynnes no peysse.

(1st Fytte, ll. 85–100)

In Scott's version, the same episode runs:

But up then spake a little page,
  Before the peep of dawn –
'O waken ye, waken ye, my good lord,
  for Percy's hard at hand.' –

'Ye lie, ye lie, ye liar loud!
  Sae loud I hear ye lie:
For Percy had not men yestreen
  To dight my men and me.

'But I have dream'd a dreary dream
  Beyond the Isle of Sky;
I saw a dead man win a fight,
  And I think that man was I.'

(ll. 65–76)

In both versions, battle is joined, and Douglas falls at Percy's hand:

The Percy was a man of strenghth,
  I tell yow in thys stounde,
He smote the Dowglas at the swordes length,
  That he felle to the growynde.
The sworde was scharpe and sore can byte,
  I tell yow in sertayne;
To the harte, he cowde hym smyte,
  Thus was the Dowglas slayne.

(2nd Fytte, ll. 105–12)

So Bishop Percy. In Scott, the theme of the dream is taken up again:

But Percy with his good broad sword,
  That could so sharply wound,
Has wounded Douglas on the brow,
  Till he fell to the ground.

Then he call'd on his little foot-page,
  And said – 'Run speedilie,
And fetch my ain dear sister's son,
  Sir Hugh Montgomery.

'My nephew good,' the Douglas said,
  What recks the death of ane!
Last night I dream'd a dreary dream,
  And I ken the day's thy ain.

'My wound is deep; I fain would sleep;
  Take thou the vanguard of the three,
And hide me by the braken bush,
  That grows on yonder lilye lee.

'O bury me by the braken bush,
  Beneath the blooming brier,
Let never living mortal ken,
  That ere a kindly Scot lies here.'

(ll. 89–104)

Douglas's body is hidden so that his men should not know of his death, and the English are defeated. Percy, acknowledging his defeat, is told by Montgomery,

Thou shalt not yield to lord nor loun,
Nor yet shalt thou yield to me;
But yield thee to the braken bush,
That grows upon yon lilye lee!

(ll. 125–8)

Eight hundred copies of the first two volumes of the *Minstrelsy* were published in 1802 and sold out within the year. They were reprinted the following year with the third volume, which consisted largely of modern versions. By 1812, in its fifth three-volume edition, it had sold about 10,000 copies.[4] With each new edition, Scott, like Percy before him, made additions and improvements to the contents. Even in 1802, the amount of money Scott made from it compared favourably with his legal fees for the year. Moreover, it brought him a degree of fame that it would have taken him a long time to earn at the Bar. His researches for it had brought him into contact with English antiquarians like Richard Heber and George Ellis and they in turn introduced him into London literary society. On his visit to London in 1803 he was mildly lionized. His future course seemed clear. In 1799 he had received his promised appointment as Sheriff of Selkirkshire, which provided him with a basic income; he was now in a position, as he said himself, where literature could be his staff but need not be his crutch.

The line of development from the *Minstrelsy* to the poems that followed is clear. *The Lay of the Last Minstrel* is, in essence, an extended ballad and is a development of the imitation ballads, many of the best of them by Scott himself, that he had published in the third volume of the *Minstrelsy*. In its early stages, it was almost certainly intended for inclusion in the third volume, but grew, Topsy-like. It is unlikely that long verse narratives like *The Lay of the Last Minstrel* and *Marmion* will ever again attain the popularity that these publications had, but in their day they were new and exhilarating (not actually entirely new; Southey had published *Thalaba* and *Madoc* but comparatively speaking they were dull, and Coleridge was working on *Christabel* but was slower off the mark[5]). As Grierson pointed out, 'all art for its effect depends to some extent on the circumstances amid which it appears.

One must throw oneself back in imagination to the time . . . when these poems appeared, to realise the freshness of the pleasure which they afforded.'[6] Scott's poems in fact outlasted the popularity of the poems of Byron, which at the time supplanted them in the public taste. They were fresh and exciting and they satisfied the gothic and medieval tastes that had been aroused by Horace Walpole, Mrs Radcliffe, and 'Monk' Lewis. The public fell on them and Scott, like Byron later, found himself famous.

The theme of *The Lay* came to Scott through the legend of Gilpin Horner, the goblin page, which had taken the fancy of the young Countess of Dalkeith, later Duchess of Buccleuch, who had asked Scott to write a ballad on the subject. It was Scott's idea to set the story within a story, putting the legend in the mouth of an ancient minstrel, the last of his profession, 'a wandering harper, scorned and poor', who is given shelter by an earlier duchess and in gratitude sings the story to her. The device adds to the length of the poem, which is probably what caused it to be unsuitable for the *Minstrelsy*; but it also gives Scott a better narrative perspective on his poem, which is rather more about the border feuding of earlier generations than about the goblin page, who becomes, as the critic Jeffrey pointed out in the *Edinburgh Review*, a perpetual burden to the poet. Even without the goblin, there is plenty of necromancy, chivalry, and raiding, and the whole thing goes at a cracking pace. It is chiefly remembered today for the minstrel's reasons for remaining in Scotland in poverty and neglect:

> Breathes there the man, with soul so dead,
> Who never to himself hath said,
> 'This is my own, my native land!
> Whose heart hath ne'er within him burn'd,
> As home his footsteps he hath turn'd,
> From wandering on a foreign strand!
> If such there be, go, mark him well;
> For him no Minstrel raptures swell;
> High though his titles, proud his name,
> Boundless his wealth as wish can claim;
> Despite those titles, power, and pelf,
> The wretch, concentred all in self,
> Living, shall forfeit fair renown,

And, doubly dying, shall go down
To the vile dust, from whence he sprung,
Unwept, unhonour'd, and unsung.

O Caledonia! Stern and wild,
Meet nurse for a poetic child!
Land of brown heath and shaggy wood,
Land of the mountain and the flood,
Land of my sires! What mortal hand
Can e'er untie the filial band
That knits me to thy rugged strand!
Still, as I view each well-known scene,
Think what is now, and what hath been,
Seems as, to me, of all bereft,
Sole friends thy woods and streams were left;
And thus I love them better still,
  Even in extremity of ill.
By Yarrow's streams still let me stray,
Though none should guide my feeble way;
Still feel the breeze down Ettrick break,
Although it chill my wither'd cheek;
Still lay my head by Teviot Stone,
Though there, forgotten and alone,
The Bard may draw his parting groan.

(Canto VI, stanzas i–ii)

The success of *The Lay* prompted Constable to offer £1,000 (over £30,000 in today's values) for *Marmion*, sight unseen, a stupendous sum for an unwritten poem and indeed a publishing innovation: as John Sutherland points out, it was not usual for publishers to offer advances in 1807, but Constable had embarked on his career as literary patron and was determined to make Edinburgh a literary mart.[7] In the event, Constable's confidence was fully justified: despite slightly mixed reviews, the poem ran through six editions in the course of the first year, and retained its popularity well into the twentieth century, with Hardy maintaining in defence of *The Iliad* that it was in the Marmion class.

Marmion is a patchy poem, the *longueurs* in it only just redeemed by the vitality of the set pieces and by the excitement of the second half and the build-up to the battle of Flodden. The battle itself, one of the most famous parts of the poem, is action poetry at its most effective:

But as they left the dark'ning heath,
More desperate grew the strife of death.
The English shafts in volleys hail'd,
In headlong charge their horse assail'd;
Front, flank, and rear, the squadrons sweep
To break the Scottish circle deep
  That fought around their King.
But yet, though thick the shafts as snow,
Though charging knights like whirlwinds go,
Though bill-men ply the ghastly blow,
  Unbroken was the ring;
The stubborn spear-men still made good
Their dark impenetrable wood,
Each stepping where his comrade stood,
  The instant that he fell.
No thought was there of dastard flight;
Link'd in the serried phalanx tight,
Groom fought like noble, squire like knight,
As fearlessly and well;
Till utter darkness closed her wing
O'er their thin host and wounded King.
Then skilful Surrey's sage commands
Led back from strife his shatter'd bands;
And from the charge they drew,
As mountain-waves, from wasted lands,
  Sweep back to ocean blue.
Then did their loss his foemen know;
Their King, their Lords, their mightiest low,
They melted from the field as snow,
When streams are swoln and south winds blow,
  Dissolves in silent dew.
Tweed's echoes heard the ceaseless plash,
  While many a broken band,
Disorder'd, through his currents dash,
  To gain the Scottish land;
To town and tower, to down and dale,
To tell red Flodden's dismal tale,
And raise the universal wail.
Tradition, legend, tune, and song,
Shall many an age that wail prolong:
Still from the sire the son shall hear
Of the stern strife, and carnage drear,
  Of Flodden's fatal field,

Where shiver'd was fair Scotland's spear,
And broken was her shield.

(Canto VI, stanza xxxiv)

Almost the most irritating part of the poem is the device by which Scott introduced each of the six cantos with verse epistles to six different friends. At one time he had considered publishing these epistles as a separate book, but abandoned this idea for reasons that are not clear. Whatever the explanation, they break up the poem abominably, and one can only sympathize with Southey, who complained that he wished them 'at the end of the volume, or at the beginning – anywhere except where they were'.[8] Ironically, the epistles, with their engaging portraits of the Scott family life, contain some of the best poetry in the whole thing, especially the landscape painting of the country round Ashestiel, where the Scotts were then living, as in the introduction to the first canto:

November's sky is chill and drear,
November's leaf is red and sear:
Late, gazing down the steepy linn
That hems our little garden in,
Low in its dark and narrow glen,
You scarce the rivulet might ken,
So thick the tangled greenwood grew,
So feeble trill'd the streamlet through:
Now, murmuring hoarse, and frequent seen
Through bush and brier, no longer green,
An angry brook, it sweeps the glade,
Brawls over rock and wide cascade,
And, foaming brown with doubled speed,
Hurries its waters to the Tweed.

(Canto I, ll. 1–14)

This is followed by tributes to Nelson and Pitt, both recently dead, culminating in the splendid tribute to Pitt:

Now is the stately column broke,
The beacon-light is quench'd in smoke,
The trumpet's silver sound is still,
The warder silent on the hill!

(Canto I, ll. 105–8)

But much in *Marmion* still justifies the enthusiasm with which it was generally received, particularly the song 'Young Lochinvar', and the scenes of the walling-up of the betrayed nun, and the vision of the ghostly voice reading out from the High Cross of Edinburgh at midnight the names of those who were to perish in the coming battle. Marmion himself is an interesting advance sketch of the character of the Templar, Brian de Bois Guilbert, in *Ivanhoe*.

Marmion was followed in 1810 by *The Lady of the Lake*, which sold over 30,000 in its first year; it also single-handed brought the tourists to the Trossachs, and supplied the United States of America with inspiration for its presidential greeting, 'Hail to the Chief'. The poem describes the struggle of James V to curb and control the power of his great nobles, who had dominated Scotland in the period of his minority (which, by the time the poem opens, he had largely done) and of the Highland chiefs and raiders who, ignoring his authority, plundered and blackmailed the Lowlands at their pleasure. Metrically, it shows an advance on the earlier poems, both in the greater ease with which he handled the octosyllabic couplets that still constitute the main part of it (what Scott called his 'light-horseman sort of stanza'), and in the less self-consciously antiquarian vocabulary. Consider, for example, the description of the nightmares of the disguised king in the island stronghold of the rebel Highland chief, Roderick Dhu:

> The hall was clear'd – the stranger's bed
> Was there of mountain heather spread,
> Where oft a hundred guests had lain,
> And dream'd their forest sports again.
> But vainly did the heath-flower shed
> Its moorland fragrance round his head;
> Not Ellen's spell had lull'd to rest
> The fever of his troubled breast.
> In broken dreams the image rose
> Of varied perils, pains, and woes;
> His steed now flounders in the brake,
> Now sinks his barge upon the lake;
> Now leader of a broken host,
> His standard falls, his honour's lost.

Then, – from my couch may heavenly might
Chase that worst phantom of the night! –
Again return'd the scenes of youth,
Of confident undoubting truth;
Again his soul he interchanged
With friends whose hearts were long estranged.
They come, in dim procession led,
The cold, the faithless, and the dead;
As warm each hand, each brow as gay,
As if they parted yesterday.
And doubt distracts him at the view,
O were his senses false or true!
Dream'd he of death, or broken vow,
Or is it all a vision now!

At length, with Ellen in a grove
He seem'd to walk, and speak of love;
She listen'd with a blush and sigh,
His suit was warm, his hopes were high.
He sought her yielded hand to clasp,
And a cold gauntlet met his grasp:
The phantom's sex was changed and gone,
Upon its head a helmet shone;
Slowly enlarged to giant size,
With darkened cheek and threatening eyes,
The grisly visage, stern and hoar,
To Ellen still a likeness bore. –
He woke, and panting with affright,
Recall'd the vision of the night.

(Canto 1, stanzas xxxiii–xxxiv)

It was to prove his most popular poem, and many lines in it are still familiar to readers who never opened it, not least the opening line, 'The stag at eve had drunk his fill'. It certainly defies the pessimism of his statement (recorded in the 1830 preface) that, if he failed in it, 'I will write prose for life'. This is an interesting indication that in 1810 he was already writing prose, and it was to be a prophetic statement, even if it was not applicable to the poem about which he said it. And the poem itself was prophetic in a way that he could not have foreseen when he wrote it, for in it he first touched on the theme that was to dominate his novels, the clash of the old culture, in this case the culture of the

Highlanders, with the new rule of law that James V was introducing in the Lowlands.

The success of *The Lady of the Lake,* together with financial embarrassments caused by family (his brothers' debts), business (the imminent insolvency of the Ballantyne publishing house in which he was now secretly a partner and in whose finances he was, unknown to almost everyone, deeply implicated), and the purchase of what was to become Abbotsford, spurred him on to his next poetic effort, *Rokeby* (published 1813). He ought not to have been financially embarrassed. He had secured an appointment as a Principal Clerk of Session, which he held in addition to his Sheriffdom, the two together ensuring him a steady income of £2,800 a year, besides the very considerable sums he had been making by his pen. But by this time he was writing to keep ahead of his liabilities. To get any kind of idea of the workload he was carrying at this time it must be remembered that, in addition to this burden of private problems and his duties as Sheriff and Clerk of Session, not to mention a very full family and social life, he was also labouring on his edition of the complete works of Swift, which eventually came out in nineteen volumes in 1814, and secretly writing the poem *The Bridal of Triermain*, which he planned to publish anonymously, simultaneously with *Rokeby*, as a spoof. And he was also working on at least one, possibly more, of the novels. What is amazing is that, under such circumstances, with the clock of insolvency and disgrace ticking loudly at his back and with the deadline for his edition of Swift overdue, he was able to write poetry at all. He complained that the poem would not come alive and tore up the first draft. Despite all these difficulties, *Rokeby,* though uneven, shows points of interesting development in his work. Set in Teesside after the Civil War battle of Marston Moor, it was the first of his poems not to have a Scottish theme and setting. Like *Marmion,* it boasted a Byronic anti-hero (though Byron's *The Bride of Abydos, The Corsair,* and *Lara* all also appeared in 1813, it is highly unlikely that Scott could have read them before *Rokeby* went to press). Most notably of all, it shows a considerable deepening in narrative skill and character drawing. As he wrote to James Ballantyne on 28 October 1812, 'knowing well that the said public will never be pleased with exactly the same thing a second time, I saw the necessity of giving a certain degree of novelty, by throwing the interest more on *character* than in my former poems, without certainly meaning to exclude either incident or description' (*L.* iii. 183-4). Of all his poems, *Rokeby* comes nearest to fiction in verse – which is perhaps hardly surprising, if it is considered that, while he was writing it, he was also secretly working on what would become *Waverley*. He was trying to make his octosyllables serve for dialogue – no easy task:

> 'It needs not. I renounce,' he said,
> 'My tutor and his deadly trade.
> Fix'd was my purpose to declare
> To Mortham, Redmond is his heir;
> To tell him in what risk he stands,
> And yield these tokens to his hands.
> Fix'd was my purpose to atone,
> Far as I may, the evil done;
> And fix'd it rests – if I survive
> This night and leave this cave alive.' –
> 'And Denzil?' – 'Let them ply the rack,
> Even till his joints and sinews crack!
> If Oswald tear him limb from limb,
> What ruth can Denzil claim from him,
> Whose thoughtless youth he led astray,
> And damn'd to this unhallow'd way?
> He school'd me, faith and vows were vain;
> Now let my master reap his gain,' –
> 'True,' answer'd Bertram, ''tis his mead;
> There's retribution in the deed.'
>
> (Canto VI, stanza xviii)

The poem did well, but financially not well enough. It would not rescue the Ballantynes and it would not pay for all he wanted to do at Abbotsford. Another poem was necessary, and in June 1813 he was asking Constable for £5,000 for what would be *The Lord of the Isles*.[9] It was published in January 1815, and did not have the immediate success of the earlier poems, though any other poet, then or later, would have been more than happy with the eventual sales. Scott, when the news of the initial disappointing reception was broken to him by the printer James Ballantyne, looked blank. Then, saying characteristically that it was more surprising that his popularity should have lasted as long as it had done than that it should have failed at last, he added 'Since one line has failed, we must just stick to something else'.[10] This was slightly disingenuous: he had already tried something else. *Waverley; or, 'Tis Sixty Years Since* had been published in July 1814.

4

The Early Novels: *Waverley* to *The Antiquary*

Scott believed that Byron had beaten him out of the field of narrative poetry 'in the description of strong passions, and in deep-seated knowledge of the human heart',[1] but he was too modest. It was not in poems like *The Bride of Abydos, The Corsair, The Giaour,* or even *Cain* that Byron's greatness consisted, nor was the author of *Old Mortality* and *The Heart of Midlothian* inferior to Byron in the description of strong passions or knowledge of the human heart. It is extremely unlikely that it was Byron's challenge that turned his thoughts to prose rather than poetry. From the outset of his career he had been looking for a medium that would give him more space and narrative freedom. His adoption of the metrical romance for *The Lay of the Last Minstrel* had been prompted by his growing distaste for the straitjacket imposed by the ballad form, and for a while this sufficed him. But the more his poems moved away from the balladic source that had originally inspired them towards storytelling, the more he found that the constraints of even the metrical romance form were still oppressive. Nowhere does this show more clearly than in *Rokeby,* where the story, which would have made a perfectly good novel, simply bursts the bounds of the container into which he poured it and tests the reader's patience to the limit. He had clearly tried his hand at prose some years earlier. He recounts, in his 1829 preface to the Magnum edition, the famous story of finding the opening chapters of *Waverley* (which he had allegedly written some years before) tucked away in the drawers of a forgotten desk when he went there to look for fishing tackle, but, as Sutherland has shown, there is a good deal of poetic licence in his account of this serendipitous discovery.[2] That the opening chapters had been written some years before is quite clear, not least from the fact that its forthcoming publication had been advertised by Longman in 1810. What had caused him to abandon the idea of finishing it then is not entirely clear, though he hints that discouragement from friends to whom he had shown the early pages was mainly responsible. It is possible that he was reluctant to hazard the reputation he had already acquired as a poet by launching out as a novelist. That this consideration still had some force when he did publish *Waverley* in 1814 is indicated by the fact that he did so anonymously; it is unlikely that this was due only to his instinctive desire to make a mystery, as he had done over *The Bridal of Triermain*. It must also be remembered that Scott was later to declare in the introduction to *The Antiquary* (when *Waverley* was a resounding success) that he had planned his first three novels to cover the period of history beginning in 1745 and continuing down to the end of the century. This, if true, must also cast a little doubt on the happy discovery of the manuscript of the first novel in an old desk drawer; it is certainly possible, to put it no higher, that parts of the novels that followed *Waverley* may have been written earlier than 1814.

The step he took in publishing *Waverley* was to be so momentous, both for him and for the future of the novel, that it should be placed in some kind of context. Scott had in his younger days been a keen reader of Fielding, Richardson, Smollett, Fanny Burney, and Henry Mackenzie, and he was also well acquainted with the gothic novels of Horace Walpole, Mrs Radcliffe, and 'Monk' Lewis.[3] Fielding he particularly admired, and he was to quote his claim 'I describe not men but manners' frequently in regard to both his poetry and his prose. Two things, each of them of less intrinsic importance than, say, his admiration for the novels of Fielding and Smollett, seem to have sparked his interest in trying fiction, one of them influencing him towards the historical novel, the other to the regional: the first was a request from the publisher John Murray in 1807 that he would complete a historical novel, *Queenhoo Hall*, left unfinished by the antiquarian and artist

Joseph Strutt, who had died in 1802; the second was the appearance of the Irish novels of Maria Edgeworth, particularly *Castle Rackrent* (1800) and *The Absentee* (1812).

Queenhoo Hall is a terrible novel, and not even Scott could make it readable. It is possibly the first real historical novel in English literature, in the sense that it tries deliberately to recreate the past for the reader – in this instance, the time of Henry VI. Scott tells us that Strutt's extensive historical studies had equipped him with all the antiquarian lore necessary for the book, but ascribes the novel's lack of success to this very fact: 'by rendering his language too ancient, and displaying his antiquarian knowledge too liberally, the ingenious author had raised up an obstacle to his own success. Every work designed for mere amusement must be expressed in language easily comprehended; and when, as is sometimes the case in *Queenhoo Hall*, the author addresses himself exclusively to the Antiquary, he must be content to be dismissed by the general reader' (*W.*, General Preface, 1829 edn.). From the beginning, and with increasing assurance as he proceeded, he understood the role of the historical novelist as mediator between the past and the present and set out his principles in the Dedicatory Epistle to *Ivanhoe*:

> It is true, that I neither can, nor do pretend, to the observation of complete accuracy, even in matters of outward costume, much less in the more important points of language and manners. But the same motive which prevents my writing the dialogue of the piece in Anglo-Saxon or in Norman-French, and which prohibits my sending forth to the public this essay printed with the types of Caxton or Wynken de Worde, prevents my attempting to confine myself within the limits of the period in which my story is laid. It is necessary, for exciting interest of any kind, that the subject assumed should be, as it were, translated into the manners, as well as the language, of the age we live in. . . . It is true that this licence is confined . . . within legitimate bounds. . . . The author . . . must introduce nothing inconsistent with the manners of the age.

In this, he makes clear the difference between what he was to do and what had hitherto been done by, for example, Horace Walpole. Regardless of where or when *The Castle of Otranto* was set, the manners portrayed are those of eighteenth-century London, just as Shakespeare's Romans are seventeenth-century

Londoners. Coleridge summed the problem up neatly in his review of Mrs Radcliffe's *Mystery of Udolpho*: 'The manners do not sufficiently coincide with the area the author has chosen; which is the latter end of the sixteenth century. There is, perhaps, no direct anachronism but the style of accomplishments given to the heroine, a country young lady, . . . give so much the air of modern manners, as is not counter-balanced by Gothic arches and antique furniture'.[4]

The second circumstance to influence *Waverley* was the work of Maria Edgeworth. Most of her educational publications would probably have been of little interest to him, but her stories of Irish life struck a chord. As the events following the French Revolution had developed ideas of nationalism that informed much of the Romantic writing in Europe, so the portrayal of cultural habits and distinctions became a subject of legitimate and popular interest. In his preface to *The Lay of the Last Minstrel*, Scott had stated that the poem 'is intended to illustrate the customs and manners, which anciently prevailed on the Borders of England and Scotland'. In his 1829 preface to *Waverley*, he writes,

> I felt that something might be attempted for my own country, of the same kind with that which Miss Edgeworth so fortunately achieved for Ireland – something which might introduce her natives to those of the sister kingdom, in a more favourable light than they had been placed hitherto, and to procure sympathy for their virtues and indulgence for their foibles.

He also thought that he might be able to exploit here his intimate acquaintance with his subject, particularly the fact of 'having had from my infancy free and unrestrained communication with all ranks of my countrymen, from the Scottish peer to the Scottish ploughman'.

The extent to which he initially followed this plan is indicated by his chapter headings in *Waverley* (he very soon abandoned the practice of using them): 'A Horse-Quarter in Scotland', 'A Scottish Manor-House Sixty Years Since', 'A Creagh and its Consequences', 'The Hold of a Highland Robber', 'The Chief and his Mansion', etc. The whole thing is as tidily laid out as a guidebook. As the story gripped him, the headings became more perfunctory, but they indicate clearly to what extent he had intended a guided tour of the Highlands, founded on his own journeys there in youth as his father's clerk and the stories to which he had listened in childhood from old Jacobites like Invernahyle. But within these limits, he was also quite clear about his intentions, which were to throw the force of the narrative 'upon the characters and passions of the actors; – those passions common to men in all stages of society, and which have alike agitated the human heart, whether it throbbed under the steel corslet of the fifteenth century, the brocaded coat of the eighteenth, or the blue frock and white dimity waistcoat of the present day' (*W.*, ch. I). *Waverley* was published on 7 July 1814 in three plain-looking12mo volumes. A thousand copies were printed. No effort was made at elegant presentation, as might presumably have been done if Scott's name had been on it, but it is clear that, from the start, he was suspected of the authorship. It sold well, and Constable had to order a reprint of 2,000 copies two days later.

Whether or not we believe Scott's claim that he deliberately planned his first three novels as a sequence, illustrating the manners of Scotland at three different periods, it is in fact what he did. But there is another point about them that is interesting, which is that there is much less pure book learning in them than there had been in his poetry. From the *Minstrelsy* onwards, the poems had been stuffed with antiquarian research. It may be that working on *Queenhoo Hall* had convinced him that antiquarian lore could be overdone. In setting *Waverley* 'sixty years since', and its successors even closer to his own day, he was placing them well within the scope of what he himself knew or had heard at first hand, from people like his grandmother and *raconteurs* like Invernahyle, and it is when he sticks to this prescription that he is greatest. Sixty years may seem a long period, but the Scots are a long-memoried people, and sixty years since in 1814 was no longer than the second World War is now from the present day. As Scott himself pointed out in the Dedicatory Epistle to *Ivanhoe,* 'many now alive . . . well remembered persons who had not only seen the celebrated Roy McGregor, but had feasted, and even fought with him. All those minute circumstances belonging to private life and domestic character, all that gives verisimilitude to a narrative, and individuality to the persons introduced, is still known and remembered in Scotland' (*I.*, p. xxvii). History impinges forcibly on the present in Scotland. Passers-by in Edinburgh still spit on the stones that mark the site of the original Heart of Midlothian, the old town jail, long demolished, and the Calvinistic disputations that figure in *Old Mortality* and *The Heart of Midlothian* could have been heard anywhere in Scotland up to the twentieth century. Throughout the eighteenth century – and Scott was in everything that mattered a child of the eighteenth century –the consequences of the Union of the Parliaments in 1707 were still being worked through and in his day were still troubling the waters. The most eminent writers in Scotland were historians – William Robertson, David Hume, Adam Ferguson, William Tytler and his son, Alexander Fraser Tytler – struggling, like their compatriots, to make sense of the changes that had been brought about, first by the Act of Union and then by the 1715 and 1745 rebellions. It is such considerations that make the dismissal of Scott as a 'mere' historical novelist so irrelevant. For him, and for many others in the Scotland of his day, in the words of William Faulkner, 'the past was not dead; it was not even past'. History threw a long shadow, and his formative years had been spent in that shadow. He had had every opportunity of observing the impact that the social and historical events of the recent past had made on characters and customs, and the lectures of the younger David Hume, which had so impressed him at university, had taught him to see these events and their effects as an organic whole.

The fruits of his observation and his historical perspective can be seen, fully developed, in his first novel. In pursuance of his intention of illustrating Highland characters and customs, he takes his young English hero, Edward Waverley, the product of a joint upbringing by a Hanoverian but absentee father and a Jacobite uncle, and sends him, as a newly recruited officer, to serve with one of King George's regiments in Scotland. While billeted there, he takes advantage of his situation to visit his uncle's old (and Jacobite) crony, the Baron Bradwardine, and to observe for himself something of Scotland north of the Highland line. During his visit, he takes the incredibly foolhardy step of going to see the lair of a Highland brigand, Donald Bean Lean, and is led from that to pay an extended visit to the (fanatically Jacobite) local chieftain, Fergus MacIvor of Glennaquoich, and his dramatically beautiful sister Flora. He falls in love with Flora, and he participates unwittingly in a gathering of the clans organized by Fergus in preparation for the 1745 rebellion. As a result of these indiscretions and a complicated sequence of events and trickery but not perhaps surprisingly, he finds that he has been cashiered from his regiment and is arrested, escapes owing to the machinations of Bradwardine's daughter Rose, and joins the army of Prince Charles Edward in a fit of pique. He participates in the battle of Prestonpans but manages to leave the insurgent army before Culloden and, through the good offices of an English officer whose life he saved at Prestonpans, he is pardoned and restored to his family and his inheritance in England. Fergus is executed at Carlisle for his part in the rebellion, Flora, who has consistently repulsed Waverley's advances, retires to a convent and Waverley marries the devoted Rose Bradwardine.

In all this, Scott had set the pattern for what was to be his most successful theme in most of his best novels. Waverley, who Scott himself cheerfully dismissed as 'a sneaking piece of imbecility', is the model for all the later Scott heroes who find themselves poised accidentally on the cusp of historical events, influenced in different directions by reason and upbringing. As with heroes like Harry Bertram, Henry Morton, Frank Osbaldistone, and many others, his apparent neutrality or colourlessness is a necessary ingredient in the novel. He is there to find the middle way between warring extremes, to provide the point of balance between the forces that are pulling in different directions, to be used as a fulcrum by the opposing parties. More importantly, he is the medium through whom events and characters can be observed. It has been pointed out that, although Scott never hesitated to introduce real historical personages into his novels (it was indeed one of his most important innovations), they are never the central characters. They would have hampered him too much and they would not have served his purpose nearly so well as the sneaking pieces of imbecility. They were better kept to the periphery. The Young Pretender, Claverhouse, Mary Queen of Scots, Cromwell, Louis XI, are magnificent portraits, but they work far better in a walk-on role. The sheer insignificance of his young heroes and heroines is important in giving him his perspective.

Through the naivety of Waverley's perceptions, the poverty and ignorance of the Highlanders can be seen; his amazement that a gentle, shy girl like Rose Bradwardine can be so matter-of-fact about the routine raids and depredations suffered by those like her father who live on the Highland line tells us much about both of them. And through his observations and reactions, we can understand the other characters, just as we can trace his own sentimental education, from his callow admiration at Waverley Honour of Miss Cecilia Stubbs (who is quickly obliterated from his mind by his commission and his new uniform), through his infatuation with the beautiful and romantic Flora MacIvor, to his more rational and enduring love for Rose. Jane Austen could not have improved on his gradual reaction to Flora's coldness:

> Upon my word, I cannot understand how I thought Flora so much – that is so *very* much – handsomer than Rose. She is taller indeed, and her manner more formed; but many people think Miss Bradwardine's more natural; and she is certainly much younger. I should think Flora is two years older than I am ... [Rose's] manner, upon the whole, is most engaging . . . She has more feeling too. (*W.*, ch. LIV)

And, just as Catherine Morland secures the affections of Henry Tilney by her open partiality for him, so Rose 'possessed an attraction which few men can resist, from the marked interest she took in everything that affected him' (*W.*, ch. LII). All the characters are realistically drawn. None is quite good or quite bad. The Baron Bradwardine is pedantic and prosy, but the irritation he arouses never conceals his real goodness of heart, his courage and integrity, and his unshakeable and uncomplaining loyalty. Evan Dhu, the type of the simple clansman who offers his life for his chief in one of the greatest scenes in the book, is one of the masterpieces of the novel; and Fergus is an arrogant, ambitious Machiavellian schemer but with so many redeeming qualities that at the end, after the high drama of the trial and execution, one can only echo the comment of Waverley's servant as they left Carlisle where the heads of both men adorned the battlements: 'It's a great pity of Evan Dhu, who was a very weel-meaning, good-natured man, to be a Hielandman; and indeed so was the Laird o'Glennaquoich too, for that matter, when he wasna in ane o' his tirrivies' (*W.*, ch. LXIX).

Waverley, with its description of the 1745 rebellion, was the first of the novels to touch explicitly on the subject of Jacobitism. Scott was to return to it in *Rob Roy*, which is set in the months leading to the 1715 rebellion, and he was to show its death throes in *Redgauntlet*, but it was in his first novel that he tackled head on what had so recently been a living issue in Scotland. It provided the ideal opportunity for writing about the oppositions that underpin most of his fiction: past versus present, civilization versus barbarism, feudalism versus democracy, and, specifically in *Waverley*, a predatory and patriarchal clan system versus constitutional government.

Throughout *Waverley*, we see a series of apparently heroic situations being collapsed by realistic punctures. The stage is set by a long (many have thought it overlong) account of Waverley's education and background, for it is essential that this should be understood in order that the reader can sympathize when he finds himself genuinely torn between opposing factions later on; and, in spite of the Jacobite sympathies of his uncle, it is clear that he enlists in the army entirely convinced of the legality of the present settlement and the benefits that the Hanoverian rulers have brought to the kingdom. He sets off for Scotland, his head stuffed with romance, to undergo his sentimental rites of passage. He is first disillusioned by finding that army life is much less glamorous, and calls for much more self-discipline, than he had fondly imagined. He is as absent and inattentive over his military duties as Fergus later finds him as a companion; he is, in fact, bored by them, and happy to make the visit to his uncle's old friend the excuse to take leave from the regiment. He arrives in the Highlands to find a series of situations and people designed exactly to fulfil his romantic ideas: the magnetism and chivalry of Fergus MacIvor, the nobility and beauty of Flora, the unfamiliar, therefore romantic customs and beliefs of Fergus's clansmen, the exploits of the outlaw, Donald Bean Lean ('some renowned outlaw, a second Robin Hood perhaps or Adam o'Gordon' (*W.*, ch. XVI) and his raids on the baron's cows, all seem calculated to meet his most exaggerated expectations. But at every step the carpet is pulled out from under him. Fergus is handsome and charismatic, but he is also manipulative and domineering. The Highlanders, Donald Bean Lean especially, are deceitful and untrustworthy. Flora pours a continual stream of cold water on his passion and his heroics ('High and perilous enterprise is not Waverley's forte', she tells Rose (*W.*, ch. LII)). Prince Charles Edward charms him initially, but not for long. One of the most telling moments in the book comes during the battle of Prestonpans, when Waverley, arrayed at the insistence of Fergus in Highland dress and serving with his clansmen, can see through the confusion of battle

> the standard of the troop he had formerly commanded, and hear the trumpets and kettle-drums sound the advance, which he had so often obeyed. He could hear, too, the well-known word given in the English dialect, by the equally well-distinguished voice of the commanding officer, for whom he had once felt so much respect. It was at that instant, that, looking around him, he saw the wild dress and appearance of his Highland associates, heard their whispers in an uncouth and unknown language, looked upon his own dress, so unlike that which he had worn from his infancy, and wished to awake from what seemed at the moment a dream, strange, horrible, and unnatural. (*W.*, ch. XLVI)

Already shaken by an encounter with the dying Houghton, sergeant of the men he had originally brought north from his uncle's estate, Waverley Honour, he is finally awoken from his dream by witnessing the death of his former commanding officer, Colonel Gardiner. The reproach of Houghton, 'Ah, squire, why did you leave us?' rings in his ears (*W.*, ch. XLV). His rescue of the English officer, Colonel Talbot, is the only recompense he can make, but it is the deed that eventually enables him to escape the consequences of his actions when Fergus and Evan are hanged.

Far from glamorizing the rebellion, Scott shows Waverley's gradual disillusionment with it, his awakening from his dreams of romance and adventure and his growing maturity. But he achieves this through his equally gradual understanding of what is going on around him, and his realization, first that the action taken by his commanding officer in cashiering him was entirely reasonable, and, secondly, that the venture in which he has enlisted in a fit of petulance is a hopeless enterprise, led by a prince who exhibits many of the characteristics that had lost his ancestors the throne, and depending for its success on an ill-led, ill-disciplined rabble army of ignorant clansmen, manipulated by chiefs such as Fergus, who are motivated by individual ambition and intrigue. They are, in fact, the direct descendants of the medieval Highlanders of Roderick Dhu in *The Lady of the Lake*, bred to rapine and violence, regarding the Lowlanders as their legitimate prey. The only leader who is depicted as truly honourable and unselfishly loyal to the house of Stuart is a Lowlander, the Baron Bradwardine; his values are those by which all the other characters are implicitly judged, although his pedantry makes him ludicrous in other ways. Thus, in his first novel, Scott sounded the theme of the opposition of romance and realism that was to recur in so many of his later novels, though rarely more effectively than it is found here. The romantic elements are persistently undercut, principally by Scott's brilliant use of dialogue – what Coleridge called 'the charm and yet the utterly impersonal and undramatic stuff and texture of the dialogue'.[5] His ear had been attuned by his employment as a lawyer and a sheriff to hearing the rhythms and vocabulary of ordinary Scots speech and here, in his first essay in fiction, he reproduces it in masterly fashion, whether it is the Lowland speech of Bailie Macwheeble or the Highland speech of Evan Dhu Mccombich when he and Fergus are condemned to death and Evan offers his life to save his chief:

> 'I was only ganging to say, my Lord' said Evan, in what he meant to be an insinuating manner, 'that if your excellent honour and the honourable court, would let Vich Ian Vohr go free just this once, and let him gae back to France, and no to trouble King George's government again, that ony six o' the very best of his clan will be willing to be justified in his stead; and if you'll just let me gae down to Glennaquoich, I'll fetch them up to ye mysell, to head or hang, and you may begin wi' me the very first man.'
>
> Notwithstanding the solemnity of the occasion, a sort of laugh was heard in the court, at the extraordinary nature of the proposal.

> The Judge checked this indecency, and Evan, looking sternly around, when the murmur abated, 'If the Saxon gentlemen are laughing,' he said, 'because a poor man, such as me, thinks my life, or the life of six of my degree, is worth that of Vich Ian Vohr, it's like enough they may be very right; but if they laugh because they think I would not keep my word and come back to redeem him, I can tell them they ken neither the heart of a Hielandman nor the honour of a gentleman.'

And when his offer is declined, 'Grace me no grace . . . since you are to shed Vich Ian Vohr's blood, the only favour I would accept from you, is – to bid them loose my hands and gie me my claymore, and bide you just a minute sitting where you are!' (*W.*, ch. LXVIII). This is speech that had not been heard in fiction before.

In *Guy Mannering* (1815), Scott moves his setting to the south-west of Scotland, in the later years of the eighteenth century, and there are no historical events in it round which he had to work. Guy Mannering, the titular hero of the novel, is very similar to Colonel Talbot in *Waverley*: both are the type of the perfect English officer, whom Scott always admired. Once again, he sends an English hero into Scotland to observe the natives but with very different results. Mannering, at the start of the book, is a young man, stormstayed on the coast of Dumfriesshire; he is sheltered at Ellangowan, the house of Godfrey Bertram, on the night when Bertram's wife is giving birth to their first child. A boy is born, and Mannering, whose hobby is astrology, casts his horoscope, which predicts that the child will encounter great danger at certain points in his life up to the age of 21. He then vanishes from the story for twenty-one years, during which time the child, Harry Bertram, is kidnapped at the age of five, the first of the danger points that Mannering had pinpointed. The story proper begins when Mannering, retired from the army, returns to settle in Dumfriesshire and arrives on the day when Godfrey Bertram, old, broken, and bankrupted, is on the point of being evicted from Ellangowan, to which there appears to be no male heir, by the villainous lawyer, Glossin, who hopes to acquire the estate for himself. Bertram and his daughter, his only remaining child, are homeless and, even as Mannering arrives, the old man dies of misery. Mannering hires a house near by and takes the daughter, Lucy, into his own home along with her grotesque and eccentric tutor, Dominie Sampson, whom he remembers from his previous visit. Almost simultaneously, the lost heir also arrives at Ellangowan, unaware of any previous connection with it, but in pursuit of Mannering's daughter Julia, whom he had loved when he was a volunteer in Mannering's regiment in India. The rest of the story concerns the unravelling of the mystery of Harry Bertram's identity with the help of characters like Dandie Dinmont, the border farmer, the lawyer Paulus Pleydell, and the gipsy Meg Merrilies.

The plot depends to some extent on the character of Godfrey Bertram, a silly, inconsequent man whose self-importance is greater than his intelligence. When he eventually contrives to get himself made a Justice of the Peace, he exercises his new responsibilities in this capacity with so little moderation that he turns his previous local popularity into deep resentment. Nowhere is this more felt than by the local smugglers, whose activities he had previously connived at, and in the colony of gipsies, which had for many years been settled at Derncleugh on the Ellangowan estate and who are given notice by Bertram to quit. He meets them on the road as they are being expelled, and is intercepted by the mother of the tribe, Meg Merrilies, who had previously been a family favourite:

> 'Ride your ways,' said the gipsy, 'ride your ways, Laird of Ellangowan – ride your ways, Godfrey Bertram! – This day have ye quenched seven smoking hearths – see if the fire in your ain parlour burn the blither for that. Ye have riven the thack off seven cottar houses – look if your ain roof-tree stand the faster. – Ye may stable your stirks in the shealings at Derncleugh – see that the hare does not couch on the hearthstane at Ellangowan. – Ride your ways, Godfrey Bertram – what do ye glower after our fold for? – There's thirty hearts there that wad hae wanted bread ere ye had wanted sunkets, and spent their lifeblood ere ye had scratched your finger. Yes – there's thirty yonder, from the auld wife of an hundred to the babe that was born last week, that ye have turned out o' their bits o' bields, to sleep with the tod and the blackcock in the muirs! – Ride your ways, Ellangowan. – Our bairns are hinging at our weary backs – look that your braw cradle at hame be the fairer spread up: not that I am wishing ill to little Harry, or

> to the babe that's yet to be born – God forbid – and make them kind to the poor, and better folk than their father! – And now ride e'en your ways; for these are the last words ye'll ever hear Meg Merrilies speak, and this is the last reise that I'll ever cut in the bonny woods of Ellangowan.' So saying, she broke the sapling she held in her hand, and flung it into the road. (*GM*, ch. VIII)

Shortly after this, Bertram's little son is kidnapped. His wife goes into premature labour with grief. She dies after giving birth to Lucy, and the fortunes of Bertram decline from that day.

Guy Mannering is a less well-constructed novel than *Waverley* (one might almost call it broken-backed), but in it, as in *Waverley*, we see the conflicting claims of two worlds – in the earlier novel, the conflict between Highlander and Lowlander, Jacobite and Hanoverian, here the conflict between the past and the present. The actions of silly, inconsequent Bertram when he becomes a JP contrast with his attitude to the smugglers when Mannering first met him:

> 'Why, Mr. Mannering, people must have brandy and tea, and there's none in the country but what comes this way – and then there's short accounts, and maybe a keg or two, or a dozen pounds left at your stable door, instead of a d–d lang account at Christmas from Duncan Robb, the grocer at Kippletringan, who has aye a sum to make up, and either wants ready money or a short-dated bill. Now Hatteraick will take wood, or he'll take bark, or he'll take barley, or he'll take just what's convenient at the time. I'll tell you a gude story about that. There was ance a laird – that's Macfie of Gudgeonford, – he had a great number of kain hens – that's hens that the tenant pays to the landlord, like a sort of rent in kind – they aye feed mine very ill.' (*GM*, ch. V)

And indeed one of the loudest complaints of the neighbouring gentry when Bertram has driven the gipsies and the smugglers out of the district is over the new difficulty in obtaining brandy and tea.

As in the previous novel there was the contrast between the old world of clan loyalties and the new world of constitutional reform, so in *Guy Mannering* there is the contrast between the old ties of loyalty and affection that united the landowners to their tenants and to the poor who depended on them, and the hard-hearted commercialism of the usurper, Glossin, who schemes to seize possession of the estate simply for what he can wring out of it. Bertram's misfortunes stem partly from his very limited intelligence but mainly from the fact that he had broken the unwritten compact that had existed between those that owned property and those who lived on it.

One mistake that Scott had made in *Waverley*, however, he avoided in *Guy Mannering*. The reader's attention in the earlier novel had been monopolized by the higher-ranking characters; the characters who give the story its salt – Baron Bradwardine, Bailie McWheeble, Davy Gellatly, and, most of all, Evan Dhu Mccombich – tend to get pushed off the page by them. In *Guy Mannering*, the story is held together by the wonderful gallery of characters who, on the contrary, tend to push the Mannerings, the Bertrams, and their lovers off the page: Dominie Sampson, Dandie Dinmont, the advocate Pleydell, and, of course, Meg Merrilies. Meg Merrilies provides the romance of the story, but Dandie Dinmont and Pleydell between them provide the robust common sense that solves the mystery in the end, and they are the ones we remember. Both of them are types that, in a sense, stand between the past and the present: Dinmont is the sturdy down-to-earth farmer who will waste money on a useless lawsuit over an acre or two of land ('a man's aye the better thought o' in our country for having been afore the feifteen' (*GM*, ch. XXXVIII)) but shows courage and generosity, not just to Harry Bertram who saved his life, but also to the little orphan maid left unprotected by the death of her mistress from whom he and others had hoped to inherit: 'And what's to come o' this poor lassie then – Jennie Gibson? Sae mony o'us as thought oursells sib to the family when the gear was parting, we may do something for her amang us surely' (*GM*, ch. XXXVIII). And he takes her back to his farm at Charlies-hope, where she will have a home with his daughters.

But the novel also excels in the portrayal of the Edinburgh of the high tide of the Enlightenment. Mannering goes there to protect Lucy Bertram's interests and falls into the hands of the advocate Paulus Pleydell, who accompanies him to the Greyfriars Kirk to hear Dr Robertson preach and supplies him with introductions to David Hume, Adam Smith, Joseph Black, John Clerk of Eldin, Lord Kaimes, and many others. Pleydell himself is a magnificent portrait of the eighteenth-century

Edinburgh advocate of the type among whom Scott had grown up and who could still have been met with in the Court of Session more than a century later: acute, humane, bibulous in his Saturday evening high jinks, 'a member of the suffering and Episcopal church of Scotland', whose library is stocked with 'the best editions of the best authors, and in particular, an admirable collection of classics. "These", said Pleydell, "are my tools of trade. A lawyer without history or literature is a mechanic, a mere working mason; if he possesses some knowledge of these, he may venture to call himself an architect"' (*GM*, ch. XXXVII).

The Antiquary (1816), Scott's own acknowledged favourite among his works, though criticized by later critics as a mish-mash of unrelated events, brings his original trio of novels up to his own day, as he had promised. The Napoleonic Wars are in progress, rumours of French invasions are in the air. The formal plot is even more far-fetched than that of *Guy Mannering*, though once again it centres on a lost heir: on this occasion one lost in darker and more Gothic circumstances, under the shadow of incest. But the machinery of the plot matters even less here than in *Guy Mannering*: the hero, Lovel, makes his entrance on the first page, but his epiphany in the final chapter as Colonel Neville, the lost heir of the Earl of Glenallan, and his rather feeble love story with Isabella Wardour, are completely overshadowed by the characters and action in the rest of the novel. The Antiquary himself, Jonathan Oldbuck of Monkbarns, is, by Scott's own admission, modelled largely on his father's old friend George Constable, from whom he had had much encouragement in his embryonic antiquarian interests in his young days, but is also in part an ironic self-portrait of Scott and his enthusiasms. John Sutherland has pointed out the biographical parallels:

> Like Scott, Oldbuck began working life as a younger brother and an apprentice to a 'writer, or attorney'. Again like Scott, he fell in love with a noble young lady, who jilted him for a better connected and richer lover. Monkbarns, like Scott, retreated into antiquarian pursuits for consolation. His father and elder brother died, as did Robert and Walter Scott WS, leaving Oldbuck a modest competence to retire on. Monkbarns is what Scott might have become had

he not, on being repulsed by Williamina, thrown himself into life with his rebound marriage to Charlotte. When as a seven-year-old boy Walter first hung on George Constable's extravagant stories, the forty-something gentleman must have seemed a figure of great antiquity. Now Scott himself was forty-something and in his old boyhood.[6]

And to cap it all, he points out the philological parallel between Monkbarns and Abbotsford. As Jonathan Oldbuck, Scott draws himself with a good-humoured self-ironizing competence: his antiquarian pedanticisms, so competently deflated by the old beggar, Edie Ochiltree ('Praetorium here, Praetorium there, I mind the bigging o't'), his pernicketiness over having his books and papers touched, his sentimental memories, his position as quartermaster of the local home guard. Much more than Colonel Mannering in the previous novel, the character of the Antiquary is the centre of the book. But even more than in *Guy Mannering*, the memorable parts of the novel are the scenes and characters that surround him. The scenes are too well integrated into the structure of the novel to be called set pieces, but they are the parts that stick in the memory, like the rescue of Sir Arthur Wardour and his daughter from Halket Head (where Scott spectacularly causes the sun to set off the east coast of Scotland) and the busybodies in the local post office:

> 'Od, here's another,' quoth Mrs Mailsetter. 'A ship-letter – post-mark, Sunderland.' All rushed to seize it. – 'Na, na, leddies,' said Mrs Mailsetter, interfering; 'I hae had eneugh o' that wark – Ken ye that Mr Mailsetter got an unco rebuke frae the secretary at Edinburgh, for a complaint that was made about the letter of Aily Bisset's that ye opened, Mrs Shortcake?'
>
> 'Me opened!' answered the spouse of the chief baker of Fairport; 'ye ken yoursell, madam, it just cam open o' free will in my hand – what could I help it? Folk suld seal wi' better wax.' (*A.*, ch. XIV)

But in the main, *The Antiquary* is concerned with people who are living in the past: Sir Arthur is in thrall to the glories of his pedigree to the extent that he cannot react practically to his present loss of fortune and imminent bankruptcy, and is fool enough to trust his remaining assets to the flattering and fraudulent adept, Dousterswivel, whom everyone else can easily see through; the Earl of Glenallan is existing in penitential misery, to expiate what he believes to have been the sin of incest in the past; even Oldbuck, with his memories of his lost love and his absorption in his antiquarian studies, is living largely in the past, though he is not incapacitated by it, as Wardour and Glenallan are, and is able to react promptly and efficiently when danger comes. These are set in contrast with the characters of lower social rank who are not paralysed by the past and are able to live in the present, like Edie Ochiltree and the Mucklebackits, especially as exemplified by the reaction of Saunders Mucklebackit, found by Oldbuck mending the boat in which his son Steenie has just been drowned:

> 'I am glad,' he said in a tone of sympathy – 'I am glad, Saunders, that you feel yourself able to make this exertion.'
>
> 'And what would ye have me to do,' answered the fisher gruffly, 'unless I wanted to see four children starve, because ane is drowned? It's weel wi' you gentles, that can sit in the house wi' handkerchers at your een when ye lose a friend; but the like o' us maun to our wark again, if our hearts were beating as hard as my hammer.' . . . At length, when he had patched a considerable rent, and was beginning to mend another, his feelings appeared altogether to derange the power of attention necessary for his work. The piece of wood which he was about to nail on was at first too long; then he sawed it off too short, then chose another equally ill adapted for the purpose. At length, throwing it down in anger, after wiping his dim eye with his quivering hand, he exclaimed, 'There is a curse either on me or on this auld black bitch of a boat, that I have hauled up high and dry, and patched and clouted sae mony years, that she might drown my poor Steenie at the end of them, an' be d——d to her!' and he flung his hammer against the boat, as if she had been the intentional cause of his misfortune. Then recollecting himself, he added, 'Yet what needs ane be angry at her, that has neither soul nor sense? She's but a rickle o' auld rotten deals nailed thegither, and warped wi' the wind and the sea – and I am a dour carle, battered by foul weather at sea and land till I am maist as senseless as hersell. She maun be mended though again the morning tide – that's a thing o' necessity.' (*A.*, ch. XXXIV)

His dignity and perseverance in his loss are contrasted with the complete abandonment of all worldly duties by the Earl of Glenallan in similar circumstances, just as the sturdy independence and robust health of the blue-gown beggar, Edie Ochiltree, is contrasted with the feebleness and decrepitude that Glenallan's useless and self-inflicted penances have brought on him. Oldbuck, the plebeian Whig, steers a canny middle course between the two extremes. He is regarded with a slightly patronizing good will, not unmixed with contempt, by the gossips of Fairport:

> 'Twa letters for Monkbarns – they're frae some o' his learned friends now; see sae close as they're written, down to the very seal – and a' to save sending a double letter – that's just like Monkbarns himsell. When he gets a frank he fills it up exact to the weight of an unce, that a carvy-seed would sink the scale – but he's ne'er a grain abune it. Weel I wot I wad be broken if I were to gie sic weight to the folk that come here to buy our pepper and brimstone, and suchlike sweetmeats.'
>
> 'He's a shabby body the laird o' Monkbarns' said Mrs Heukbane; 'he'll make as muckle about buying a forequarter o' lamb in August as about a back sey o'beef'. (*A.*, ch. XV)

In spite of the comedy of scenes like this, and of Edie's and Steenie's persecution of Dousterswivel and of Hector's encounter with the seal, there is a curiously ominous atmosphere looming over the whole book; it implies a threat from the future, not entirely related to the shadows cast by the past. The country is at war, social unrest is in the air, there is a general feeling of insecurity and of the vanity of human wishes. One is reminded, again and again, of Scott's deep admiration for Samuel Johnson.

5

The Later Novels

In his first three novels, Scott had given a remarkably comprehensive outline of the issues that were to preoccupy him for the remainder of his writing career, and his subsequent work, fiction and non-fiction, was to confirm what he had already laid down as his themes. Some, perhaps, were to emerge more clearly in later work. In *Old Mortality*, possibly his greatest novel, certainly one of his grimmest, he was to return in much greater detail to the subject of fanaticism, which he had touched on much more slightly in *Waverley*. There, the fanaticism of Fergus MacIvor for the Jacobite cause is to some extent lost in the rest of the story, though it is perceptibly there and is indeed, in Fergus's unscrupulous manipulations of Waverley, the mainspring of the plot. In *Old Mortality*, it was to take centre stage.

This was also the first novel in which Scott was to take a step backwards in time. In his first three, he had been dealing with periods barely outside his own experience: 1745, about 1770, and the 1790s. *Old Mortality* goes back to 1679, nearly 100 years before his birth, and, like *Waverley*, its action is dictated by real historical events: the brutal assassination by the more extreme Covenanters of Archbishop Sharpe of St Andrews in May 1679, the subsequent skirmish at Drumclog on 1 June in which the Covenanting insurgents managed to rout the government forces led by John Graham of Claverhouse, and the battle of Bothwell Bridge in which the Covenanting army was comprehensively defeated on 22 June. The main action of the novel therefore takes place within a space of little more than a month, and, though there is a postscript set about ten years later, required to resolve the love story and dispose of the remaining characters, it is nonetheless one of the most tightly plotted of Scott's novels, and the one in which, once the opening chapters have been disposed of, the reader's attention is most completely gripped.

The hero, Henry Morton, is a more adult and more intelligent version of Waverley, placed in a similarly ambiguous situation through much less fault of his own. It is set in a period (the background is important) when the memory of the repressive Cromwellian invasion of Scotland was still fresh, and the swing of the pendulum to the more liberal and indeed libertine regime of the Restoration was in full swing. The Cromwellian annexation of Scotland had been bitterly resented, but it had had the effect of confirming the fanatical religious domination of the extreme Calvinists or Covenanters, and these were now, under Charles II and the restored Episcopalian Church, correspondingly persecuted. 'I have been for some time of opinion', says one of the characters, 'that our politicians and prelates have driven matters to a painful extremity in this country, and have alienated, by violence of various kinds, not only the lower classes, but all those in the upper ranks, whom strong party-feeling, or a desire of court-interest, does not attach to their standard' (*OM*, ch. XXIV). Henry Morton, who has been brought up by a miserly and narrow-minded uncle (who, in so far as he inclines to any side, inclines to the Covenanters or Whigs) and who does not come into either of these categories, finds himself obliged to give shelter to an old army comrade of his dead father who is now on the run. For refusing to betray his whereabouts to the detachment of dragoons commanded by Sergeant Bothwell, who come in search of him, he is himself arrested. Until this point, he has not been aware that the fugitive, Balfour of Burley, was the ringleader of the assassins of Archbishop Sharpe, a crime that revolts him even more than the careless brutality and licentiousness of the government soldiers. He is taken to the nearby Castle of Tillietudlem, a Royalist stronghold that had held out in the recent wars for the king, to await the judgement of the commanding officer, Graham of Claverhouse. Tillietudlem is now the home of the widowed Lady Margaret Bellenden and her granddaughter, Edith Bellenden, with whom Morton is hopelessly in love. Claverhouse orders

Morton to be shot instantly, but his life is spared by the intercession of Lord Evandale, a Royalist officer who is also in love with Edith, and he is taken, still prisoner, by Claverhouse with his forces to confront the Covenanting insurgents who are reported to be under arms at Drumclog. Here Claverhouse is defeated, and, in the rout of his forces, Morton is abandoned and taken by the Covenanters, whom he joins, hoping to be influential in presenting a reasonable and convincing protest against the abuses of the time to the government. He becomes one of their leaders and joins with them in besieging the Castle of Tillietudlem, partly in the hope of being able to protect Edith and her grandmother in the event of the castle falling. But his tenderness to the malignants (as the Covenanters term the Royalists) is perceived, and, by the machinations of Balfour of Burley, he is sent off on a mission as the siege reaches a critical stage. He returns in time to find that Evandale, who had been defending the castle, has been taken and is on the point of being shot, and that the castle has been reduced by starvation to the point of surrender. He rescues Evandale, to the indignation of Burley, and escorts the Bellendens to safety.

By this time, the defeat of Claverhouse at Drumclog has aroused the government to the seriousness of the situation, and the Duke of Monmouth, at the head of a much larger force, is on the march to meet the rebel army. Morton, with the more moderate of the insurgents, draws up and presents to him a list of the grievances and demands of the rebels, but Monmouth, while approving its reasonableness, will treat with them only if they will first lay down their arms. This offer is refused, the Battle of Bothwell Bridge takes place, and the Covenanters are routed. Morton's life is spared through the joint petitions of Evandale and Claverhouse, who has been impressed by his conduct, though he is exiled from Scotland. Burley escapes, but the rest of the rebels are executed. Ten years later, after the Revolution of 1688, Morton is able to return to Scotland, where he finds that the Bellendens have been reduced to misery and poverty by the machinations of Burley, who, after the surrender of Tillietudlem, had removed from the castle various documents that were necessary to establish their title to the property, and that Edith, believing him to be dead, is on the point of marrying Evandale. He seeks out Burley, now insane, with the intention of forcing him to surrender the documents, but without success. Burley contrives the murder of Evandale, who dies, joining the hands of Edith and Morton, and is himself killed during his escape.

The mere outline of the plot gives no impression of the darkness and urgency of the narrative. The action starts at the game of the popinjay at the wappenschaw or muster in Lanarkshire, and one feels instinctively, though it is not stated, that it is a typical Scottish May, the kind of May castigated by William Dunbar – not wholesome nor benign. Morton returns from it to the cold and sordid parsimony of his uncle's house, meeting Burley on the way; he shelters him in a stable overnight, but sends him away in the morning for his own safety as soon as he can see to distinguish his track through the morasses. The ground on which the rebels take their stand at Drumclog is marshy and broken, scattered with straggling alders 'too much dwarfed by the sour soil and the stagnant bog-water to ascend into trees' (*OM*, ch. XIV) (the novel was written during one of the wettest summers on record in Scotland). There is none of the dash and gallantry in the battle scenes that is found in *Marmion* or *Waverley*: the fighting is hard, bloody, and brutal. The frequent interruptions of the action by the devotions and preaching of the Covenanters and their clergy add to the inspissated gloom of the atmosphere. The comedy provided by Cuddie Headrigg, Morton's Sancho Panza, has little chance of lightening it.

The novel climaxes on two final horrors. The first is the scene in which Morton sits in a deserted farmhouse, surrounded by his former comrades, who blame him for their defeat at Bothwell Bridge, waiting for the striking of the clock to mark the end of the Sabbath when they will shoot him. This scene reaches a climax of balladic intensity as Claverhouse appears at the last minute:

> 'Hist,' [Mucklewrath] said – 'I hear a distant noise.'
>
> 'It is the rushing of the brook over the pebbles,' said one.
>
> 'It is the sough of the wind among the bracken,' said another.
>
> 'It is the galloping of horse,' said Morton to himself, his sense of hearing rendered acute by the dreadful situation in which he stood. – 'God grant they may come as my deliverers.' (*OM*, ch. XXXII)

The second is the trial and torture before the Privy Council of the Cameronian preacher, Ephraim Macbriar. Macbriar, who has refused to reveal the hiding-place of Burley, is dragged away to the scaffold; Morton is exiled. The heroism of Macbriar cancels out to some extent the horror of the earlier scene in which he had also been involved as one of the would-be executioners.

Throughout the novel, Morton, a very much more positive character than Waverley, stands between the figures of Claverhouse and Burley, equidistant from the fanaticism of each. He sympathizes with the grievances of the Covenanters, but, even more, he is revolted by the state of affairs he sees around him. 'I am weary,' he says, 'of seeing nothing but violence and fury around me, – now assuming the mask of lawful authority, now taking that of religious zeal' (*OM*, ch. V). His efforts to steer a moderate and moderating course between extremes earn him the suspicion of both sides. He plays in the novel the role that is played by someone in almost all the Waverley novels, not just the nondescript but necessary hero but the voice of common sense, the voice, almost, of posterity. It is a voice that is heard in many of the novels, and not only from the hero. 'Will future ages believe that such stupid bigotry ever existed?' exclaims the wicked Templar in *Ivanhoe*, inveighing against the superstition of the Grand Master of the Temple (*I.*, ch. XXXVI). Morton, rescued by Claverhouse, hears with horror the shots of the firing squad that kill most of his would-be assassins:

> 'You are but young in these matters, Mr Morton,' said Claverhouse, after he had very composedly finished his draught; 'and I do not think the worse of you as a young soldier for appearing to feel them acutely. But habit, duty, and necessity, reconcile men to everything.'
>
> 'I trust,' said Morton, 'they will never reconcile me to such scenes as these.'
>
> 'You would hardly believe,' said Claverhouse in reply, 'that, in the beginning of my military career, I had as much aversion to seeing blood spilt as ever man felt – it seemed to me to be wrung from my own heart; and yet, if you trust one of those whig fellows, he will tell you I drink a warm cup of it every morning before I breakfast. But in truth, Mr Morton, why should we care so much for death, light upon us or around us whenever it may? Men die

daily – not a bell tolls the hour but it is the death-note of some one or other; and why hesitate to shorten the span of others, or take over-anxious care to prolong our own? It is all a lottery. – When the hour of midnight came, you were to die – it has struck, you are alive and safe, and the lot has fallen on those fellows who were to murder you. It is not the expiring pang that is worth thinking of in an event that must happen one day, and may befall us on any given moment – it is the memory which the soldier leaves behind him, like the long train of light that follows the sinking sun – that is all which is worth caring for, which distinguishes the death of the brave or the ignoble.' (*OM*, ch. XXXIII)

The pursuit of fame and honour is Claverhouse's form of fanaticism; Burley's religious variety is darker and more dangerous, and yet oddly similar:

'Young man,' returned Balfour, 'you are already weary of me, and would be yet more so, perchance, did you know the task upon which I have been lately put. And I wonder not that it should be so, for there are times when I am weary of myself. Think you not it is a sore trial for flesh and blood, to be called upon to execute the righteous judgments of Heaven while we are yet in the body, and continue to retain that blinded sense and sympathy for carnal suffering, which makes our own flesh thrill when we strike a gash upon the body of another? And think you, that when some prime tyrant has been removed from his place, that the instruments of his punishment can at all times look back on their share in his downfall with firm and unshaken nerves? Must they not sometimes even question the truth of that inspiration which they have felt and acted under? – must they not sometimes doubt the origin of that strong impulse with which their prayers for heavenly direction under difficulties have been inwardly answered and confirmed, and confuse, in their disturbed apprehensions, the responses of Truth itself with some strong delusion of the enemy?'

'These are subjects, Mr Balfour, on which I am ill qualified to converse with you,' answered Morton; 'but I own I should strongly doubt the origin of any inspiration which seemed to dictate a line of conduct contrary to those feelings of natural humanity which Heaven has assigned to us as the general law of our conduct.' (*OM*, ch. V)

Claverhouse recognizes the similarity in fanaticism between them, but distinguishes between 'the blood of learned and reverend prelates and scholars, of gallant soldiers and noble gentlemen, and the red puddle that stagnates in the veins of psalm-singing mechanics, crack-brained demagogues, and sullen boors' (*OM*, ch. XXXIV). 'God gives every spark of life, – that of the peasant as well as of the prince,' is Morton's answer.

The final section of the novel, when Morton returns after a ten-year absence, cannot be other than a slight anti-climax, and the twist in the plot, by which Burley has contrived to deprive the Bellenden ladies of their home and inheritance, is unconvincing. It is dictated purely by the need to tie a few knots, to unite Morton and Edith, to provide a suitably heroic death for Lord Evandale, and to dispose of Burley. But there are memorable moments in it, as when Edith, discussing wedding arrangements with Evandale, sees what she takes to be the ghost of Morton walking past the window, and the final scene between Morton and Burley, the latter by now a raving lunatic.

An incidentally interesting aspect of the novel, however, concerns not its content but its presentation. Scott, always prone to secrecy, retreats in it behind yet further veils of mystification. *Waverley* had been published anonymously: the next two novels were advertised as 'by the author of *Waverley*'. His next novels were to appear under the title *Tales of my Landlord*, the first series of which comprised *The Black Dwarf* and *Old Mortality*, and were ascribed to a pedantic schoolmaster, Jedediah Cleishbotham (*anglicé* Thwackum). The reasons for this further obfuscation are not clear. Sutherland ascribes it to Scott's amusement at the 'Diedrich Knickerbocker' persona created by Washington Irving for his *History of New York* (1809), and to his desire to be able, by creating a variety of pen names, to deal profitably with other publishers than Constable, who had published the first three novels and naturally looked forward to publishing others.[1] It is certainly the case that, at this stage, Scott was playing a number of publishers off against each other, and at this point was negotiating simultaneously, apart from Constable, with Longman and John Murray in London and William Blackwood in Edinburgh. As usual, he needed to raise more cash, for Abbotsford and to clear off old borrowings. But he could have done all this, and indeed more profitably, under the banner of 'the author of *Waverley*' than under a completely new pseudonym. As Constable dejectedly pointed out, the history of Scotland that Scott offered to him as an anonymous publication would have sold many copies with his name on it. Without it, he could not hope to sell more than 2,000. Scott did not like to feel himself in the power of a single publisher, but he did want to make profitable deals. It seems yet another instance of his innate love of secrecy.

Whatever his motives, the first series of *Tales* was offered, through the usual medium of James Ballantyne, to William Blackwood (who clearly deduced without too much effort who Ballantyne's anonymous principal was). What Scott was proposing was a series of four one-volume novels, set in the four corners of Scotland, 'illustrative of ancient Scottish manners and of the traditions of their respective districts'. *The Black Dwarf*, set in the Liddesdale hills and inspired by the tales of Border raids to which he had listened with such fascination as a child, represented the south of Scotland; *Old Mortality* the west. The novels depicting the north and east never materialized, at least not in the form that Scott had originally intended. Instead, *Old Mortality* swelled to three volumes instead of the projected one, thus fulfilling his contract with Blackwood in quantity if not in content. *The Black Dwarf* has never been a popular novel, though it has more points of interest than have sometimes been admitted, not least in its treatment of lameness. But Scott himself admitted that he had 'tired of the ground I had trode so often, so I quarrelled with my story and bungled up a conclusion' (*L.* iv. 291). *Old Mortality* was triumphantly successful. But the layers of obscurity in which Scott envoloped this latest of his personae do not, for modern readers at least, contribute to that success. The device of the author of *Waverley* (because there was in fact no real doubt as to his responsibility) ascribing the authorship to Jedediah Cleishbotham, who in turn is transcribing and presenting the manuscript of his friend Peter Pattieson, who is himself recounting the story he has been told by the former Covenanter, known locally as Old Mortality, who had made it his self-appointed task to travel the district, cleaning and repairing the tombstones of the covenanting martyrs, makes for the most awkward and irritating opening chapter that any great novel has ever been burdened with, and must have deterred many youthful or not very determined readers. Sutherland suggests that 'Chinese Whispers' might have been a more appropriate title. The opening sentence of the introduction to *Tales of my Landlord,* which is put in the mouth of Cleishbotham, is probably the most offputting start to any novel yet invented:

> As I may, without vanity, presume that the name and official description prefixed to this Proem will secure it, from the sedate and reflecting part of mankind, to whom only I would be understood to address myself, such attention as is due to the sedulous instructor of youth, and the careful performer of Sabbath duties, I will forbear to hold up a candle to the daylight, or to point out to the judicious those recommendations of my labours which they must necessarily anticipate from the perusal of the title-page.

When Scott prepared the novel for reprint in the Magnum edition (where it did not appear until 1833, after his death), he remedied the defect to some extent by turning the first chapter into a 'Preliminary' so that chapter 2 became chapter 1; but undid any advantage he might have gained from this device by adding a new 'Introduction' with more information about the legend of Robert Paterson, or Old Mortality. It is from this point in his career that we may date Scott's habit of encumbering the opening of his novels in this way. The Jedediah Cleishbotham expedient brought other inconveniences in its wake, since it provoked the advertisement some years later of a fraudulent 'Fourth series of *Tales of my Landlord*'; it is noticeable that after this attempt at piracy, Scott made little real attempt to hide the author of *Waverley* behind any other fictional personae and, in his introductory epistle to *The Fortunes of Nigel*, abandoned any such attempt completely.

At all events, with his next novel Scott returned to a more orthodox arrangement with Constable, and *Rob Roy* appeared credited to 'the author of *Waverley*'. It was written while he was suffering from the first of his severe and agonizing attacks of gallstones, for which he had been subjected to almost equally agonizing medical treatment and large quantities of opium, which had reduced him almost to a skeleton. None of this shows in the work, which is one of Scott's most delightful.

In *Rob Roy,* although it is set in an earlier period than *Waverley* (1715 as opposed to 1745), Scott writes his real requiem for the old clan society of the Highlands. The combination of the Act of Union of 1707 between Scotland and England and the Hanoverian settlement had produced a society in Scotland in which it could no longer survive. In 1816 Scott had written an article for the *Quarterly* on the Culloden papers, in which he had delivered the verdict, 'Clanship, however, with its good and evil, is now no more'. In *Rob Roy*, he provides his fictional rationalization of this statement and his justification of the Act of Union.

> 'Whisht, sir! – whisht! [Bailie Nicol Jarvie rebukes Andrew Fairservice.] It's ill-scraped tongues like yours, that make mischief atween neighbourhoods and nations. There's naething sae gude on this side o' time but it might hae been better, and that may be said o' the Union. Nane were keener against it than the Glasgow folk, wi' their rabblings and their risings and their mobs, as they ca' them now-a-days. But it's an ill wind blaws naebody gude . . . Now, since St Mungo catched herrings in the Clyde, what was ever like to gar us flourish like the sugar and tobacco trade? Will onybody tell me that, and grumble at the treaty that opened us a road west-awa' yonder?' (*RR*, ch. XXVII)

The whole novel is a celebration of the commercial enterprise that the Hanoverian succession and Whig prosperity had made possible and a recognition that, in this new order, the old patriarchal culture, whether in the form of clan society in the Highlands of Scotland or in the Jacobite squirarchy in the north of England, was doomed. The Bailie, who is the real hero of the novel and the prototype of the new, wealthy mercantile class that had been made possible in Scotland by the 1707 Union, provides a succinct and convincing analysis of the economic situation in Scotland:

> 'Ye are to understand, that the Hielands hae been keepit quiet since the year aughty-nine – that was Killiecrankie year. But how hae they been keepit quiet, think ye? By siller, Mr Owen – by siller, Mr Osbaldistone. King William caused Breadalbane distribute twenty thousand gude punds sterling amang them, and it's said the auld Hieland Earl keepit a lang lug o't in his ain sporran. And then Queen Anne, that's dead, gae the chiefs bits o' pensions, sae they had wherewith to support their gillies and caterans that work nae wark, as I said afore; and they lay by quiet eneugh, saving some spreagherie on the Lowlands, whilk is their use and wont, and some cutting o' thrapples amang themsells, that

> nae civilised body kens or cares onything anent. – Weel, but there's a new warld come up wi' this King George (I say God bless him, for ane) – there's neither like to be siller nor pensions gaun amang them; they haena the means of mainteening the clans that eat them up, as ye may guess frae what I said before; their credit's gane in the Lowlands; and a man that can whistle ye up a thousand or feifteen hundred linking lads to do his will, wad hardly get fifty punds on his band at the Cross o' Glasgow. – This canna stand lang – there will be an outbreak for the Stuarts – there will be an outbreak – they will come down on the low country like a flood, as they did in the waefu' wars o' Montrose, and that will be seen and heard tell o' ere a twelmonth gangs round.' (*RR*, ch. XXVI)

The 1715 rebellion starts at the end of the novel, justifying the Bailie's acumen.

The novel starts with a typical Scott hero, Frank Osbaldistone, scorning a place in his father's mercantile business because he wishes to be a poet (he is, like Scott, an admirer of Ariosto). His father, William Osbaldistone (Protestant Whig), disinherits him, banishes him to Osbaldistone Hall, the Northumberland estate of his elder brother, Sir Hildebrand Osbaldistone (Catholic Tory), and offers the place to Sir Hildebrand's youngest son, Rashleigh, instead. Frank, arrived in Northumberland, finds Sir Hildebrand and his six sons (with the exception of Rashleigh) stupid, illiterate, gluttonous, and hunting mad. Rashleigh, who had been designed for the priesthood, is not stupid and illiterate but devious and deceitful. The only compensation for the uncongenial company in which he finds himself is Sir Hildebrand's niece, Diana Vernon, who is living at Osbaldistone Hall in circumstances that Frank finds mysterious. As soon as he arrives at the Hall, Frank finds himself embroiled in a series of embarrassing and potentially damaging misadventures, which he ascribes to the malice of Rashleigh, who, soon after his arrival at the Hall, left it to take up the place in his uncle's house in London. Rashleigh establishes himself in his uncle's confidence and is left in charge of the office during the elder Osbaldistone's absence on business abroad. Frank receives a letter from his father's partner (from which he finds that earlier correspondence between him and his father had been suppressed), informing him that Rashleigh, while in charge of the office, had absconded to Scotland with papers that would ruin Frank's father if they were not recovered before certain bills fell due. Frank rushes off to Scotland, attended by the garrulous and impertinent Scots gardener, Andrew Fairservice, and with a mysterious letter of introduction given to him by Diana Vernon.

By the time Frank reaches Scotland, the reader is halfway through the book, and still at a loss to find any connection between the content and the title. On Frank's arrival in Glasgow, however, he discovers that his father's head clerk, Owen, who had also gone to Scotland to recover the lost papers, has been thrown into jail and that a mysterious cattle-drover who has figured in some of his adventures so far, and who takes him to visit Owen in jail, is the mysterious Highland robber, Rob Roy, to whom Diana's letter of introduction had been directed. In the jail, the extremely respectable Bailie Nicol Jarvie turns up to rescue Owen, and is revealed to be the far-removed cousin of Rob Roy through 'the auld wife ayont the fire at Stuckavrallachan'. An appointment is made for the Bailie and Frank Osbaldistone to meet Rob Roy over the Highland line at the Clachan of Aberfoil, where he will help them to recover the missing papers. The remainder of the book is occupied by the consequent adventures in the Highlands, the foiling of the plots of Rashleigh (who turns out to be in the pay of the Old Pretender and had designed to rob Frank's father for his benefit), and the outbreak of the 1715 rebellion. Sir Hildebrand and his remaining sons are disposed of in a page, and Frank returns dutifully to his father's counting house, inherits Osbaldistone Hall, and marries Diana.

As a plot, it is not a miracle of construction, and it is riddled with absurdities, not the least of which is why, having been disinherited at the outset and therefore presumably at his own disposal, Frank agrees to be immured in the uncongenial surroundings of Osbaldistone Hall – and, indeed, why his father should send him to a place where he could derive so little benefit. There is also the peculiarity of Rashleigh's earning so high a degree of trust in a very few weeks that he is left in charge of the business, not only over the experienced chief clerk, Owen, but over the managing director's partner, who was sufficiently active in the business to write to Frank to warn him of what was going on. The annihilation of Sir Hildebrand and his five other sons is so offhand as to arouse a combination of fury and hilarity. And yet the momentum of the plot carries it all off. This is partly due to the masterful characterization, which, in this novel, is managed with such balance and artistry that there is no exaggeration or slack. Frank is the usual nondescript hero, less effective even than Waverley, but somehow we believe in his passion for Diana Vernon in a way that we never could in Waverley's for Flora. The scene in which they part on the hillside, as they believe for ever, is memorable and the answer to critics who maintain that Scott could never write a convincing love scene. And, in Diana, Scott achieved his most successful heroine so far, beautiful and witty, a direct descendant of Shakespeare's Beatrice. Even Frank's father, who makes only token appearances at the beginning and end of the novel, is a fully believable personality, and additionally interesting for the light he casts on Scott's perception of his own situation at this time, as he manipulated printing and publishing companies and speculated in landed property:

> In the fluctuations of mercantile speculation, there is something captivating to the adventurer, even independent of the hope of gain. He who embarks on that fickle sea, requires to possess the skill of the pilot and the fortitude of the navigator, and after all may be wrecked and lost, unless the gales of fortune breathe in his favour. This mixture of necessary attention and inevitable hazard, – the frequent and awful uncertainty whether prudence shall overcome fortune, or fortune baffle the schemes of prudence, affords full occupation for the powers, as well as for the feelings of the mind, and trade has all the fascination of gambling without its moral guilt. (*RR*, ch. I)

In an age when gentlemen did not engage in trade, Scott, the would-be landed gentleman, justifies to himself through Mr Osbaldistone his own engagement in the mercantile pursuits which he kept well hidden from his friends.

But the triumph of the novel (and this may be due in part to Scott's preoccupation in it with the idea of the dignity of commerce) is the character of Bailie Nicol Jarvie. He comes before us first at second hand, in Owen's description of him to

Frank, by contrast with the smooth and obliging rival firm of McVittie and Macfin (who will throw him in jail), as

> a man whose good opinion of himself amounted to self-conceit, and who, disliking the English in general as much as my father did the Scotch, would hold no communication but on a footing of absolute equality; jealous, moreover; captious occasionally; as tenacious of his own opinions in point of form as Owen could be of his; and totally indifferent though the authority of all Lombard street had stood against his own private opinion. (*RR*, ch. XXII)

We meet him at first hand in the unforgettable scene in the Glasgow jail, when, the Sabbath safely over, he turns out at midnight to do what he can for the distressed Owen, just as opinionated and self-important and canny as reputed, but with an efficiency and willingness to help that even survives his discovery of Rob Roy in the jail, – 'ye robber – ye cateran – ye born deevil that ye are, to a' bad ends and nae gude ane – can this be you?' (*RR*, ch. XXIII). And from there he dominates the story, accompanying Frank into the Highlands both to help him and to recover the thousand pounds scots he had lent Rob Roy years before. In this novel he takes over the role of holding the middle ground between extreme factions that is usually held by the titular hero, for he is the sane centre of the whole book, and his company and his conversation are a constant delight.

The 1715 rebellion plays no such major part in *Rob Roy* as the 1745 rebellion did in *Waverley*. The emphasis is on different themes, and the main theme is the contrast between the prosperity and the productivity of the commerce that is carried on in London and Glasgow and the desolation of the Highlands, where half a village of 1,000 souls may be employed,

> 'wi' some chance of sour-milk and crowdie; but I wad be glad to ken what the other five hunder are to do?'
>
> 'In the name of God!' said I, 'what *do* they do, Mr Jarvie? It makes me shudder to think of their situation.'
>
> 'Sir,' replied the Bailie, 'ye wad maybe shudder mair if ye were living near hand them. For, admitting that the tae half of them may make some little thing for themsells honestly . . . ye hae still mony hundreds and thousands o' lang-legged Hieland gillies that will neither work nor want, and maun gang thigging and sorning about

on their acquaintance or live by doing the laird's bidding, be't right or be't wrang. (*RR*, ch. XXVI)

Scott knew well that the old order of the Highlands was finished; but he is quite clear also about the injustices and hardships that the new order imposed on their inhabitants, and about the ignorance and indifference in London that caused them. He did not live to see the Highland clearances; but they would not have surprised him, though he would have deplored them. As Arnold Kettle pointed out, Scott's knowledge of poverty, despite his Toryism, was not simply academic.[2]

He was to come back once more to the subject of Jacobitism in his last really fine novel, *Redgauntlet* (1824), his final return to the period and the subjects in which he was most at home and most successful. In this he writes of a non-historical rising that never took place in the second half of the eighteenth century, not long after the coronation of George III. It was a hopeless attempt to fan the embers of an anachronistic movement, whose adherents had long settled for compromise with the House of Hanover, and for surreptitious passings of wine glasses over water jugs in toasts to the king over the water. History had moved on; you cannot bathe in the same river twice. The gentry whom Redgauntlet summons to the banner of Charles Edward would not really have welcomed a Stuart restoration; they had too much to lose. Their dismay at finding their romantic nostalgia for the old line taken literally and they themselves required to stake their lives and estates for a pretender who, Scott takes care to demonstrate, displays all the worst features of the late Stuart kings is amusing. All can see this except Redgauntlet himself, a fanatic who might have been a rather more idealistic Fergus MacIvor in middle age. The finest scene in the book is towards the end, when the Hanoverian General Campbell, who has arrived with a regiment of soldiers, walks into the room where the conspirators and the Pretender are agitatedly discussing what to do next, and suggests that they should all go quietly home.

'Is this real?' said Redgauntlet. 'Can you mean this? – Am I – are all, or any, of these gentlemen at liberty, without interruption, to

> embark in yonder brig, which I see is now again approaching the shore?'
>
> 'You, sir – all – any of the gentlemen present,' said the General – 'all whom the vessel can contain are at liberty to embark uninterrupted by me; but I advise none to go off who have not powerful reasons, unconnected with the present meeting, for this will be remembered against no one.'
>
> 'Then, gentlemen,' said Redgauntlet, clasping his hands together as the words burst from him, 'the cause is lost for ever!' (*R.*, ch. XXXVI)

It is indeed lost, for they are not worth arresting or putting on trial, not even the Young Pretender, who is now merely an embarrassment to his Hanoverian cousin in London. It is one of the finest examples in Scott of the mediation of the past into the present, the heroics punctured by realism, comedy, and a degree of fatalism.

There is a subsidiary but important interest in *Redgauntlet*, which is the appearance in it of what is possibly the first modern short story in English literature, 'Wandering Willie's Tale'. The ancestry of the short story in the British Isles is long and complicated, but the short story as it is known today, and more particularly the ghost story, has a relatively short history, and in this specimen it springs, fully formed, from its creator's head, spine-chilling, perfectly constructed as a story in its own right, but beautifully incorporated into the structure of the novel of which it forms a part. The debt it owes to the ballads of sorcery and superstition that Scott had included in his *Minstrelsy* is clear, but this is a straightforward, perfect specimen of the genre, in which the piper of the Redgauntlet family visits his dead master in hell to get from him the receipt for the rent he had paid him before he died, which will save him from eviction. It is the direct ancestor of Stevenson's 'Thrawn Janet'. Scott was to return to the short story later in his *Chronicles of the Canongate* (1827), the first series of which consisted of three stories, 'The Surgeon's Daughter', 'The Highland Widow', and 'The Two Drovers', and again later with 'My Aunt Margaret's Mirror' and 'The Tapestried Chamber'.

The Heart of Midlothian (1818 and assigned once again to Jedediah Cleishbotham) is a completely different type of novel from *Rob Roy*, but oddly starts from a similar point, although here the emphasis is less on economics and more on law. It is set in 1736, nearly thirty years after the Union of the Crowns, and the encroachments of Westminster, now that the first flush of financial advantage celebrated by the Bailie is fading, are bearing hard on the citizens of Edinburgh. The opening scene describes the historical Porteous riots. Porteous, the captain of the city guard, has fired upon the public at the execution of a notorious smuggler, and killed several; for giving this order, he is condemned to death, but is reprieved at the last moment by order of Queen Caroline, and to the fury of the citizens of Edinburgh.

> 'I am judging,' said Mr Plumdamas, 'that this reprieve wadna stand gude in the auld Scots law, when the kingdom *was* a kingdom'.
>
> 'I dinna ken muckle about the law,' answered Mrs Howden; 'but I ken, when we had a king, and a chancellor, and parliament-men o' our ain, we could aye peeble them wi' stanes when they werena gude bairns – But naebody's nails can reach the length o' Lunnon.'
>
> 'Weary on Lunnon, and a' that e'er came out o' t!' said Miss Grizel Damahoy, an ancient seamstress; 'they hae taen awa our parliament, and they hae oppressed our trade. Our gentles will hardly allow that a Scots needle can sew ruffles on a sark, or lace on an owerlay.'
>
> 'Ye may say that, Miss Damahoy, and I ken o' them that hae gotten raisins frae Lunnon by forpits at ance,' responded Plumdamas; 'and then sic an host of idle English gaugers and excisemen as hae come down to vex and torment us, that an honest man canna fetch sae muckle as a bit anker o' brandy frae Leith to the Lawnmarket, but he's like to be rubbit o' the very gudes he's bought and paid for. – Weel, I winna justify Andrew Wilson for pitting hands on what wasna his; but if he took nae mair than his ain, there's an awfu' difference between that and the fact this man stands for.' (*HM*, ch. IV)

Wilson's fellow-smuggler, Robertson, inflames these feelings still further to raise a mob to storm the tollbooth, known as the Heart of Midlothian, liberate the prisoners, drag out Porteous, and hang him. For this act of rebellion, the outraged Queen exacts a heavy fine and deprives Edinburgh of its civic privileges.

Scott links the historical event of the riot with his plot through the device of making one of the prisoners in the Heart of Midlothian a girl, Effie Deans, who had been seduced by Robertson and borne him a child, which has disappeared. Under the law, she is accused of child murder because she concealed her pregnancy, did not summon help in her labour, and cannot account for the child's whereabouts; Robertson presses her to use the storming of the tollbooth to escape, but she refuses. After the lynching of Porteous, she duly stands trial and is condemned to be hanged. In the inflamed political situation, there is no hope of a royal pardon for her, despite the jury's recommendation of mercy. The crucial point of the trial is whether she told her half-sister, Jeanie Deans, of her situation; if she had done so, she would not have been guilty of concealing her pregnancy.

So far the issue, as regards both Porteous and Effie, has been the law of the land and its application to specific crimes: in particular, in Porteous's case, the law of England as it applies in Scotland. With the entry into the plot of Jeanie Deans and her father, David Deans, the emphasis shifts from the law of man to the law of God. David Deans is an old Covenanter of the *Old Mortality* school, who had fought at Bothwell Bridge: his elder daughter, Jeanie, has been brought up in strict adherence to his rigid beliefs. Effie, panicking, not unnaturally, at the sentence that hangs over her, begs her sister to testify at the trial that she had told her of her pregnancy. Jeanie, equally appalled at the prospect of committing perjury, is torn between saving her sister's life and committing what she believes to be a mortal sin. Her father, seeing his daughter's dilemma, believes that she can honestly swear to having known of the pregnancy but thinks that her hesitation comes (as his would do) from her unwillingness to testify in the court of law of a government that has not signed the Solemn League and Covenant, to him as dire an offence as perjury. Nevertheless, his concern for his younger child causes him to urge her to do this if her conscience will permit her:

> '. . . questionless, this act may be in the opinion of some a transgression, since he who beareth witness unlawfully, and against his conscience, doth in some sort bear false witness against

his neighbour. Yet in matters of compliance, the guilt lieth not in the compliance sae muckle, as in the mind and conscience of him that doth comply. . . . Jeanie, if ye can, wi' God and gude conscience speak in favour of this puir unhappy' – (here his voice faltered) – 'She is your sister in the flesh – worthless and cast-away as she is, she is the daughter of a saint in heaven . . .' (*HM*, ch. XXIV)

Jeanie does not realize that her father's scruples as to her witness arise from his belief that the idea of testifying in an uncovenanted court of law is as serious a matter to her as it would be to him. She therefore believes that, in urging her to appear at the trial, as he does, he is encouraging her to commit perjury, and her distress is commensurately increased. The climax comes in the court scene when Jeanie, questioned on oath, bursts out, 'Alack! Alack! She never breathed word to me about it,' and the shock causes the old man to collapse. This is the high point of the novel: when 'the accumulated tensions – sister against sister, humanity against legalism, puritanism against worldliness, extreme presbyterianism against the episcopalian tradition, peasantry against town, Scotland against England – are all in play'.[3]

The scruples that torture Jeanie and urge her on her walk to London to plead with the Queen for Effie's life do not command instant sympathy in the twenty-first century any more than Isabella's do in *Measure for Measure*. The telling of a white lie to save the life of a sister whom she knew to be innocent would not now be regarded as particularly heinous, nor, if Scott is to be believed, would it have been so regarded in eighteenth-century Edinburgh. But the tragic choice that Jeanie has to make is as real to her as Isabella's (or indeed as Antigone's), and it is because she is so convincingly drawn and her torment of mind so well understood that the principles that rule her become live issues to the reader. As it is, from the scene in court, the tension gradually declines, and most readers wish that the final volume, which shows David Deans and Jeanie and her husband comfortably settled on the estate of the Duke of Argyle, had never been written. After the trial, even the cast of supporting characters, such as the two Lairds of Dumbiedykes and Ratcliffe the jailer, recede into the distance; Effie's lover, Robertson, revealed as Sir George

Staunton and increasingly prominent as Jeanie travels through England, is a poor substitute for them. Neither Madge Wildfire nor her hellcat mother is as good as Meg Merrilies. It is Jeanie's character that carries the novel; it is Scott's triumph that, out of a dairymaid of little beauty, no wit, and rigid piety, he is able to fashion a heroine who can, through the power of love and resolution, make the more extreme rigidity of Calvinism acceptable. There is nothing heroic about Jeanie; in England, her Scottish country habits and her uncompromising religious observances stick out like a sore thumb. But they make her a real person.

Apart from *Redgauntlet, The Heart of Midlothian* was the last of Scott's novels in which he was to use material in which he was thoroughly at home, in which he could examine at first hand the effect of the historical process on older cultures and societies and codes of behaviour that he knew well. The nearest he got to it thereafter was in *The Bride of Lammermoor* (1819), a curious phenomenon, written at a time of severe illness when his life was despaired of. Scott claimed that he had written or dictated most of it under the influence of opium, so that, when he saw it printed, he remembered nothing of it. His illness was certainly real, but it has now been proved that four-fifths of the manuscript is written in his normal hand, with no sign of the severe pain that he was suffering, though the opium may well have affected his memory. Whatever the truth of the method or time of composition (and there are anachronistic peculiarities in it that do point to some confusion of mind), there is no doubt that it is in many ways a sport in the series of *Waverley* novels. In the first place, it is an unmitigated tragedy, unleavened by humour or hope (Ravenswood's servant, Caleb Balderstone, is not funny enough to count). In the second, it is far and away the most poetic of all his prose works. It reads almost like a ballad, with the constant refrain of predestinate doom echoing through it in a way that happens nowhere else in his fiction: '[Lucy's] life had hitherto flowed on in a uniform and gentle tenor, and happy for her had not its present smoothness of current resembled that of the stream as it glides downwards to the waterfall!' (*BL*, ch. III); 'But Providence had prepared a dreadful requital for this keen observer of human passions' (*BL*, ch. XVI); 'the real charms of the daughter, joined to the supposed services of the father, cancelled in his memory the vows of vengeance which he had taken so deeply on the eve of his father's funeral. But they had been heard and registered in the book of fate' (*BL*, ch. XVII). It recalls the description of Heorot in *Beowulf*: 'the hall towered, high and wide-gabled, awaiting the battle-flames, the hostile fire'. It is gothic in a way none of Scott's other novels is, the plot bedevilled by ill-fated prophecies, blind seers, ruined castles, gravediggers, and wicked mothers. It is full of set pieces that might have come straight from Walpole or Mrs Radcliffe:

> the apartment was suddenly illuminated by a flash of lightning, which seemed absolutely to swallow the darkness of the hall. Every object might have been for an instant seen distinctly. The slight and half-sinking form of Lucy Ashton, the well-proportioned and stately figure of Ravenswood, his dark features, and the fiery, yet irresolute expression of his eyes, – the old arms and scutcheons which hung on the walls of the apartment, were for an instant distinctly visible to the Keeper by a strong red brilliant glare of light. (*BL*, ch. X)

It is not clear which year Scott thought he was setting the story in. From the context, it must have been fairly soon after the Union of the Parliaments in 1707 (when it became possible to appeal from the Court of Session in Edinburgh to the House of Lords in London), and while the impact of the Union on the Scottish judicial system was still shaking down into place.[4] The true story on which Scott based it took place shortly before the Union. But here again the plot centres on the opposition of tradition and progress. The family of Ravenswood is heroic but stuck in the past (although the Master of Ravenswood tries vainly to shake off his inherited shackles); the Ashtons, husband and wife, are venal and devious but they represent the present and the new realities; they live according to Wordsworth's poem on Rob Roy's grave, 'That they should take who have the power, and they should keep who can'. Ravenswood is the Master of Ravenswood, but not for nothing is Sir William Ashton, Lord Keeper of the Great Seal of Scotland, always referred to as the Keeper. The unfortunate

Lucy is caught between the opposing parties. The Whigs and Tories, jostling in the background, are equally corrupt and greedy. One of the really significant points in the novel is the passage where the gravedigger, a former Ravenswood tenant, curses the Ravenswood family:

> '. . . when they had lands and power, they were ill guides of them baith, and now their head's down, there's few cares how lang they may be of lifting it again.'
>
> 'If Lord Ravenswood protected his people, my friend, while he had the means of doing so, I think they might spare his memory,' replied the Master.
>
> 'Ye are welcome to your ain opinion, sir,' said the sexton; 'but ye winna persuade me that he did his duty, either to himsell or to huz puir creatures, in guiding us the gate he has done – he might hae gien us liferent tacks of our bits o' houses and yards – and me, that's an auld man, living in yon miserable cabin, and John Smith in my dainty bit mailing, and his window glazen, and a' because Ravenswood guided his gear like a fule!'
>
> 'It is but too true,' said Ravenswood, conscience-struck; 'the penalties of extravagance extend far beyond the prodigal's own sufferings.' (*BL*, ch. XXIV)

It is, however, an astonishingly tightly constructed novel, moving without loss of impetus (after the usual prolix opening chapter of explanation by Jedediah Cleishbotham) from Ravenswood's first encounter with Lucy and her father to the final catastrophe. There is a break of twelve months in the middle during which Ravenswood is abroad on some very improbable diplomatic duties and Lady Ashton is working to force her daughter to break her engagement with him, but it barely breaks the continuity and flow of the story. From the moment of his return it moves with the inevitability of a landslide to the final cataclysm. Scott had taken his plot from the real-life story of a daughter of the Earl of Stair, who, like Lucy, had been separated from the man to whom she had pledged herself, been forced to marry another man, and had gone mad on her wedding night, stabbing her husband almost to death. He followed it closely, even using some of the words that occur in the original version (which he gives in his 1830 preface) in his own novel, and this may have contributed to the force and urgency of the narrative. There is no force or urgency in Lucy Ashton, whose passivity of character is well portrayed in the song she sings, one of Scott's best lyrics:

> Look thou not on beauty's charming,
> Sit thou still when kings are arming,
> Taste not when the wine-cup glistens,
> Speak not when the people listens,
> Stop thine ear against the singer,
> From the red gold keep thy finger,
> Vacant heart, and hand, and eye,
> Easy live and quiet die.
>
> (*BL*, ch. III)

So often many of the best of Scott's lyrics occur not in his narrative poems but inserted, like this one, in the texture of his novels, like 'Proud Maisie' in *The Heart of Midlothian* and Rebecca's hymn 'When Israel, of the Lord beloved' in *Ivanhoe*. Even in the long poems, it is most often the songs sung by the characters in them that stick longest in the memory – 'Jock of Hazeldean', 'Bonny Dundee', 'Where shall the lover rest'.

After *The Bride of Lammermoor* (and indeed in the same year), Scott left his own territory and plunged into medieval England, inventing as his ostensible author in his first venture, *Ivanhoe*, the lawyer, Laurence Templeton. His story is set in the reign, or rather absence of reign, of Richard Cœur de Lion, and for it he produced in his dedicatory epistle his most considered essay yet on the writing of historical fiction:

> What I have applied to language, is still more justly applicable to sentiments and manners. The passions, the sources from which these must spring in all their modifications, are generally the same in all ranks and conditions, all countries and ages; and it follows, as a matter of course, that the opinions, habits of thinking, and actions, however influenced by the peculiar state of society, must still, upon the whole, bear a strong resemblance to each other.

He went on to compare the art of the historical novelist with the imagination of a landscape artist:

> It is true that this licence is confined in either case within legitimate bounds. The painter must introduce no ornament inconsistent with

> the climate or country of his landscape; he must not plant cypress-trees upon Inch-Merrin, or Scottish firs among the ruins of Persepolis; and the author lies under a corresponding restraint. However far he may venture in a more full detail of passions and feelings, than is to be found in the ancient compositions which he imitates, he must introduce nothing inconsistent with the manners of the age.

Scott himself was to violate this last prescription conspicuously in *Ivanhoe*, when he writes of one character 'starting up as if electrified'; but the very attention that this anachronism has attracted is itself an indication of how rare such lapses were with him. What he wanted was language that (unlike that used by Strutt) would be intelligible to all readers, yet would by carefully controlled archaisms convey a sense of distance from the period in which it was set, and in this he succeeded. Thus was tushery born.

Ivanhoe has always been one of the most popular of Scott's novels; ironically, it tends also to be the one that, since it is often the only one known, most forms the reader's view that Scott is not a writer worth taking seriously. For those who know his other work, it is clear that many of his most important themes are to be found in it, particularly the reconciliation of a divided society and consciousness of nationality, but it would be idle to pretend that it is not, first and foremost, a first-rate adventure story, with the advantage of one of Scott's best heroines in the Jewess Rebecca (to whom he has the resolution not to give a conventional happy ending), and a well-constructed plot that pivots on three main episodes: the tournament at Ashby de la Zouche, the siege of Torquilstone Castle, and the final encounter between Ivanhoe and the Templar to save Rebecca from being burnt at the stake.

From the success of *Ivanhoe* (which was considerable) Scott went on to other periods and other settings, some more successful than others, none totally without interest, even if only of an accidental kind. In this accidental category may be put his anticipation in *The Talisman* of one of the favourite tricks of later detective fiction, when Richard Cœur de Lion demands of the villain that he should

> '. . . deny the accusation which this mute animal hath in his noble instinct brought against thee, of injury done to him, and foul scorn to England?'
>
> 'I never touched the banner,' said Conrade, hastily.
>
> 'Thy words betray thee, Conrade!' said Richard; 'for how didst thou know, save from conscious guilt, that the question is concerning the banner?' (*T.*, ch. XXIV)

Apart from coining a device for which later authors were to be grateful, there is much of interest in Scott's approach to Saladin, the Crusades, and the Middle East in general that was to influence later writers, as has been pointed out by Robert Irwin.[5] *The Fair Maid of Perth*, which, apart from some fine action writing, is undoubtedly Scott's bloodiest novel, reeking of gore from start to finish, produces the phenomenon of a heroine who, in one of the most sanguinary periods of Scottish history, announces without any apparent sense of the ridiculous that she cannot bear the sight of blood. And in *The Fortunes of Nigel*, *Quentin Durward*, and *Woodstock*, he created in James VI, Louis XI of France, and Oliver Cromwell three of the most memorable portraits of real-life characters that the historical novel has ever produced. In *Woodstock* in particular, written under the combined stress of his financial ruin and his wife's death, there is, apart from the portrait of Cromwell, the character of Sir Henry Lee, an ageing baronet, ruined and lonely, attended only by his daughter and allowed to remain in his ancestral home only on sufferance, into whose creation it is not too fanciful to suppose that he poured much of his own suffering.

6

Catastrophe and *The Journal*

From the moment Scott began publishing until the day of his final ruin, his life had appeared to flow on in a steady course of prosperity and happiness. Surrounded by family and friends, he had appeared to most of his acquaintance the child of good fortune. His legal career gave him security and a congenial life; his literary career gave him fame and wealth beyond the dreams of avarice. Abbotsford was rising about him, the outward and visible symbol of his success. At the outset of his career, the loss of his first love, Williamina Belsches, to a better-born and more prosperous rival had, in his own words, left a crack in his heart that had never entirely healed, though it had been 'handsomely pieced'. Too much can be made of Scott's early disappointment; his deep affection for Charlotte Carpenter, whom he married very shortly afterwards, cannot be doubted, nor his happiness in his family life with her and their children. From the moment of his marriage, he seems never to have looked aside from the path of strict fidelity, nor to have been tempted to. He had early accepted the fact that he was unlikely to prosper at the bar as an advocate, but had so arranged matters, with his sheriffdom and his post as Principal Clerk of Session, that it was unnecessary that he should do so. His legal work gave him ample time for writing and for the country life that he enjoyed.

Beneath the surface, things were not entirely as they seemed. His early friendship with the Ballantyne brothers at Kelso had gradually developed into business ties that had involved him in a secret existence as partner, first in James Ballantyne and Co., printers, and then in John Ballantyne and Co., publishers. The loss of face that he would have suffered if this secret existence had become known is hard to understand now but was very real then. It is difficult to understand the motivation that drove him to this double life; he had always had an instinctive aversion to becoming the 'property' of any individual publisher, even Constable, who treated him generously, and he found the Ballantynes useful intermediaries and negotiators in his dealings with the book trade, referring to John Ballantyne as his 'brilliant little haggler'. They were also essential to preserving the secret of his authorship of the novels from 1814 onwards, and complicated routines were devised, which involved secret copying of original manuscripts and proof corrections in the printing house so that his distinctive handwriting should not be seen and recognized. They and Constable were the only professionals who were in the secret of the author of *Waverley*, and, as time went on, he became more and more dependent on James Ballantyne especially, who not only organized all the copying routines and printed all his work but also acted as his editor and critic.

Scott, however, who was so astute in gauging the public taste in his own work, proved less reliable when choosing the works to be produced by Johnny Ballantyne's publishing house. He consulted his own enthusiasms and preferences too much and overestimated the likelihood of sales. His enthusiasm for the work of the dramatist Joanna Baillie was not shared by the book-buying public; and, in the case of the *Edinburgh Annual Register*, which was intended to be the Scottish version of the English *Annual Register*, and was to have been the foundation stone of the publishing house, he set it up with great enthusiasm but designed it on too grandiose a scale, and simply underestimated the amount of work that would be required to execute it. In the event, it proved a foundation stone that dragged the enterprise under water and drowned it. By 1813, John Ballantyne and Co. was in bad trouble, the bank was refusing credit, and bills were falling due. Scott was obliged to borrow to meet obligations (without, of course, revealing what the money was for) if he was not to be revealed to Edinburgh and the world as a bankrupt tradesman. It did not help matters that Scott had bought Abbotsford in 1811 and had by 1813 embarked on his ambitious programme of rebuilding. The publishing house was wound up, with the assistance of loans raised by Scott and some help from Constable, who was, of course, anxious to rivet Scott to his own house as tightly as possible. The whole business, as Scott himself acknowledged frankly later, was, or should have been, a salutary warning to him: 'I had a lesson in 1814 which should have done good upon me, but success and abundance erased it from my mind', he wrote in his journal in 1825, when the final catastrophe was descending on him (*J.* 10, 22 Nov. 1825). In the meantime, he continued a partner in James Ballantyne and Co. Lockhart comments on the extraordinary spectacle of a man 'who could persist, however mechanically, in noting down every shilling that he actually drew from his purse,' but who 'should have allowed others to pledge his credit, year after year, upon sheafs of accommodation paper, "the time for paying which up, must certainly come", without keeping any efficient watch on their proceedings – without knowing, any one Christmas, for how many thousands, or rather tens of thousands, he was responsible as *a printer in the Canongate!*'[1]

The whole question of the financial dealings that were eventually to overwhelm Scott, Ballantyne, and Constable is immensely complicated: so much so that, when Grierson came to write his biography, he relied heavily on the help of an accountant who had devoted years to unravelling the spider's web of transactions between them and between Constable and the firms with which he dealt. There is little doubt, however, that, although Constable might have been pulled down in the crash that came in 1825, it is possible that James Ballantyne and Co. might have survived if it had been better capitalized and better run. It had full order books and was, as far as printing went, a competent firm. The real problem was that the partners in it drew on it for their private expenses as if it were an inexhaustible bank, and reinvested nothing; it was a particular problem that Scott drew on it in advance of books that he had not yet written. As the trustee for Scott's estate, John Gibson WS, was to write in 1833, after his death, 'I found it utterly impossible from the Books to discover how the accounts of the partners really stood. There was no account between them entered in the Books and neither they nor any other person could have told how much each had drawn from the concern' (*L.* i, p. lxxx).

In the meantime, however, the crisis of 1813 was surmounted, and life continued as it had done before. Scott was helped to forget the warning he had had by a natural optimism to which he was always prone where money was concerned. The novels poured out in an apparently unstoppable stream, financing the rising walls and expanding grounds of Abbotsford. It was much more important to him than any novel; it was his romance in stone. As Shakespeare dreamed of his coat of arms and the best house in Stratford, so Scott dreamed of Abbotsford and planting trees. To speak of it as an unworthy extravagance, as Carlyle did when he spoke of Scott writing daily 'with the ardour of a steam-engine that he might make £15,000 a year and buy upholstery with it',[2] is to miss the point. As Scott wrote in his introduction to *Rokeby*,

> it had been an early wish of mine to connect myself with my mother-earth and prosecute those experiments by which a species of creative power is exercised over the face of nature. . . . With the satisfaction of having attained the fulfilment of an early and long-cherished hope, I commenced my improvements, as delighted in their progress as those of the child who first makes a dress for a new doll.

He himself described Abbotsford as his Delilah and admits that land was his extravagance, but he did not build or buy to make a vulgar show. Land was as sensible an investment then as it would be now, for a man who was earning the equivalent today of £350,000 a year. He was not extravagant in other ways (except perhaps over books), and his personal tastes were simple. If it be true, as Johnson maintained, that a man is rarely more innocently employed than in making money, there are surely few more innocent ways of spending it than on establishing a country estate that gave pleasure to himself and employment to many. He was a progressive landowner, welcoming innovations such as the new railway (he invested in the Melrose branch of the Kelso to Berwick line), which he thought would bring prosperity to the district. During the depression of 1819, instead of dismissing any of the Abbotsford workers, he created new jobs in road making, forestry, and a new sawmill, which would absorb surplus labour. His patriarchal approach to the relationship between master and servant is out of fashion today, but it was infinitely preferable then to the purely cash nexus that operated in the big cities. Scott has been branded a romantic Tory escapist, mostly by those who have not read him, but he was a romantic only in a limited sense and an escapist in no sense at all. He may have built a mock-baronial mansion, but he was the first man in Scotland to install gas lighting in his home and to try out a novel system of bells that worked by air compression (and that still works today). His Toryism never prevented him from recognizing the evils that industrial workers suffered when they had been drawn from the country to the town to work for long hours and poor pay and then abandoned when the work they had come to do ended. On the other hand, he was not blind to the evils caused by the exploitation of the poor by the old families, as he shows by the words he puts in the mouth of Mrs Christie Steele in *Chronicles of the Canongate*:

> 'They did little good; they lifted their rents and spent them, called in their kain and eat them. . . . Maybe on a winter day [the tenants] wad be called out to beat the wood for cocks or siclike, and then the starving weans would maybe get a bit of broken bread, and maybe no, just as the butler was in humour – that was a' they got'. (*CC*, ch. IV)

And in the same chapter:

> 'Ye maun ken little of the warld, sir, if ye dinna ken that the health of the poor man's body, as weel as his youth and strength, are all at the command of the rich man's purse. There never was a trade so unhealthy yet, but men would fight to get wark at it for twa pennies a day aboon the common wage.'

These are not the words of a romantic escapist. He took pride in providing good working conditions on his own estate, and when his good times came to an end and bankruptcy stared him in the face, it was as much for his tenants as for himself that he grieved: 'poor Will Laidlaw – poor Tom Purdie – this will be news to wring your heart and many a poor fellow's besides to whom my prosperity was daily bread' (*J.* 47–8, 18 Dec. 1825). And, in political terms, his early exposure to the romantic Jacobite stories of Invernahyle and his father's other Jacobite clients never seduced him from his conviction that the Hanoverian establishment was infinitely preferable for the prosperity and peace of the country, however unromantic individual representatives of it (such as George IV) might be: 'I am sure such a character is fitter for us than a man who would long to head armies or be perpetually intermeddling with *La grande politique*' (*J.* 249, 20 Oct. 1826).

The high point of Scott's life probably came between 1820 and 1824. He was, as always, running a race to keep ahead of his creditors and he had genuinely no idea that Constable's firm was as insecurely based as it actually was. Long before the crash, Constable's partner, Cadell, realized that their one hope of surviving was to keep Scott writing, to keep the novels coming. 'Our most productive culture is the Author of *Waverley*' he wrote to Constable on 6 June 1822. 'Let us dig on and dig on at that extraordinary quarry – and as sure as I now write to you we will do well – but if we embark on the Sea of miscellaneous adventure and sacrifice the great gains on that Author's books for the picking small points we will only repent when it is too late' (*L.* vii. 179 n.). Indeed, it is clear that Cadell went to considerable lengths to cover up from Scott how precarious Constable's affairs were.

But Scott, the incurable optimist, was easily fooled in financial matters. In 1820 he was created a baronet by the new George IV and married his elder daughter, Sophia, to John Gibson Lockhart, a briefless advocate (as he had been himself in the past) but a clever young man of letters who had been creating scandal in the columns of *Blackwood's Magazine*. Abbotsford was approaching completion, and in 1821 he masterminded the state visit of the new monarch to his northern kingdom, dressing him, a Sassenach king, in tartan to symbolize the unified state of the Highlands and Lowlands of Scotland, a condition that they had certainly never achieved under any previous monarch either before or after the union with England. The domestic life at Abbotsford exhibited an almost idyllic perfection: he himself enjoying better health than he had had for some years, his children filling the house with life, the young Lockharts installed in Chiefswood, a cottage on the Abbotsford estate, the birth of his first grandchild, a constant flow of visitors, ceaseless schemes for occupation and diversion. And through it all, he still found time to write. In the years between 1820 and 1824, in spite of his court work, non-stop entertainment, and his improvements at Abbotsford, nine novels were published.

Redgauntlet, published in 1824, was the last of the really great novels. In 1825, the first chill winds began to blow. Lady Scott's health was failing, his sons had left home, the Lockharts left for London, where his son-in-law was to edit the *Quarterly Review*, and only his younger daughter, Anne, was left. Towards the end of the year, the preliminary rumblings of the great financial crash that was brewing could be heard, with rumours of the failure of Hurst and Robinson, Constable's London correspondents. Labour on his *Life of Napoleon*, Constable's last grandiose scheme, was hard and to some extent uncongenial, and he was also working on *Woodstock*. In November, he started on what to many is his greatest literary accomplishment, his Journal.

It has been suggested that the idea of a journal was given to him by Pepys's diaries, which he had been reading to review them in the summer of 1825. Journals can be of many kinds and Scott's tells us much about the man. He began it just before the Lockharts' departure for London in December, and that in itself indicates something about his motives for embarking on it. He was going to miss them more than he was prepared to admit, even to himself. Neither of his sons, even if they had been in Edinburgh, was of a literary turn of mind; he could talk to Lockhart about things he could talk to no one else about. Openly, he ascribes his resolution to the influence of Byron's journal, which he had just seen: 'I have bethought me . . . that he probably had hit upon the right way of keeping such a memorandum-book by throwing aside all pretence to regularity and order and marking down events just as they occurd to recollection. I will try this plan and behold I have a handsome lockd volume . . .' (*J.* 3, 20 Nov. 1825).

The day after this first entry, he writes, 'I am enamourd of my Journal. I wish the zeal may but last' (*J.* 5), and indeed it lasted, with few intermissions, until an undated entry in April 1832 when, on his return from Naples to Rome in his final visit to Italy, he writes 'We slept reasonably but on the next morning . . .' (*J.* 800) and made no further entries. Between 1825 and 1832 it became to him an indispensable companion and confidant. To begin with, there is a little catching-up feeling about it, as he goes back in recollection over his summer's visit to Ireland and his impressions of the Irish, and talks in greater detail about friends whose names have happened to occur to him than he would do later. But almost immediately, on 22 November, he noted events that jolt him sharply into the present:

> Here is matter for a May morning. But much fitter for a November one. The general distress in the city has affected H[urst] and R[obinson], Constable's great agents. Should they *go*, it is not likely that Constable can stand, and such an event would lead to great distress and perplexity on the part of J[ames] B[allantyne] and myself. Thank God I have enough at worst to pay 40/- in the pound taking matters at the very worst. (*J.* 10)

It is clear that Scott realized, if not from the outset, then at least fairly soon, that the journal would probably be published, though not in his own lifetime; even before the crash, it was understood that Lockhart would eventually write his life, and he had already supplied him with notes on his early life to help him to do so. After the crash, it became clear that anything he wrote had monetary value and would have to be exploited for the benefit of his creditors. He also explicitly set himself a rule of not erasing anything he had written. This takes a good deal of courage; not many people would happily take a vow of non-erasure in anything destined eventually for publication, especially anything as intimate as a journal, but the very few deletions noted by the journal's editor show how honourably he kept it. If he had not been so continually pressed for time during the years he was writing it, there might have been more temptation to look back and correct or alter. (He does, occasionally, go back not so much to correct as to supplement – for example, after an entry in which he records that, after a bad fall when coming home at night, he has decided to use his coach in future, much though he dislikes doing so. A note has been written in beside this entry, 'Within eight weeks after recording this graceful act of submission I found I was unable to keep a carriage' (*J.* 17, 25 Nov. 1825).) In fact, as it goes on, it seems more and more as though, for the most part, he had forgotten he was doing anything more than talking to himself, or to guests round the dining-room table, except that he could say to his journal what he could not have said to guests. And it is fairly certain that not even his most intimate family would have known what he wrote in it. The admissions of bad health, poor spirits, and financial anxiety could not have been made to anyone else. Lockhart described it with some reason as 'perhaps the most candid Diary that ever man penned'. That he had been feeling the need for a private confessional of this nature for some time may be indicated by the comments of Darsie Latimer on his journal writing in *Redgauntlet*:

> at last I have gained so much privacy as to enable me to continue my Journal. It has become a sort of task of duty to me, without the discharge of which I do not feel that the business of the day is performed. True, no friendly eye may ever look upon these labours, which have amused the solitary hours of an unhappy prisoner. Yet, in the meanwhile, the exercise of the pen seems to act as a sedative upon my own agitated thoughts and tumultuous passions. I never lay it down but I rise stronger in resolution, more ardent in hope. A thousand vague fears, wild expectations, and indigested schemes, hurry through one's thoughts in seasons of doubt and of danger. But by arresting them as they flit across the mind, by throwing them on paper, and even by that mechanical act compelling ourselves to consider them with scrupulous and minute attention, we may perhaps escape becoming the dupes of our own excited imagination; just as a young horse is cured of the vice of starting, by being made to stand still and look for some time without any interruption at the cause of its terror. (*R.*, ch. XXII)

Apart from his increasing need to have somewhere to express himself privately and openly, it is probable that Scott was also feeling the need for a different medium of expression. Just as he had outgrown the ballad form and the metrical romance in finding his true voice in the novel, so now he was beginning to feel that he had exhausted even the possibilities of the novel, at least as far as he himself was concerned. During Tom Moore's visit to Abbotsford in October 1825, Scott, speaking about the Waverley novels, had said to him, 'They have been a mine of wealth to me – but I find I fail in them now – I can no longer make them so good as at first'.[3] It was certainly one reason why he embarked on the life of Napoleon, saying to Constable, 'Often, of late, have I felt that the vein of fiction was nearly worked out; often, as you all know, have I been seriously thinking of turning my hand to history.'[4] But Napoleon, as he expanded from the scale originally conceived to the eventual nine volumes, turned out to be hard labour: Lockhart tells us that 'he read, and noted, and indexed with the pertinacity of some pale compiler in the British Museum', emerging from his toil over it with 'aching brow, and eyes on which the dimness of years had begun to plant some specks, before they were subjected again to that straining over small print and difficult manuscript'.[5] His journal was a welcome respite from such labours.

Whatever his motivation in starting on it, it turned into what he could not have foreseen, his most moving and memorable work. He started it a worldwide celebrity, at the peak of his powers, surrounded by an affectionate family, happy, successful, and (he believed) wealthy. Within months, he had lost his wife, his fortune, his reputation, and, he believed initially, his home. Sutherland believes that 'in these appallingly humiliating circumstances it evidently became more important than ever that he should preserve a noble image of himself *in extremis* for posterity'.[6] He would not have been human if there had not been an element at least of self-justification in his mind. But it is not possible to read the record of 1825–6 particularly and be unmoved by the pain, grief, and courage in it. The first intimations of the crash came, as we have seen, within days of his starting it; there followed all the doubtful consolations of false hope, good resolutions for the future ('No more Building. No purchases of Land till times are quite safe. No buying books or expensive trifles – I mean to any extent. And Clearing off encumbrances with the returns of this year's labour' (*J.* 18, 25 Nov. 1825). It must be remembered that the financial crash did not only affect the publishing world; it was a national disaster in which English banks (not Scots ones, interestingly) and many much bigger businesses than Constable and Ballantyne went down, and in the tail wave of which they were caught up, willy-nilly.

In the meantime, he had the departure of the Lockharts for London to regret ('To-day is Sunday when they always dined with us and generally met a family friend or two. But we are no longer to expect them' (*J.* 22, 27 Nov. 1825)), and he worried about the impression Lockhart would make in London; he feared his Hidalgo air and his character as a satirist would put people off. Most of all, he was anxious about his little grandson, who had been born with a spinal disease. His own sight was going and his lameness was becoming more of a handicap ('such things must come and be received with cheerful submission . . . I have perhaps all my life set an undue value on these gifts' (*J.* 26, 30 Nov. 1825). In spite of these troubles, he could say:

> I have much to comfort me in the present aspect of my family. My eldest son independent in fortune united to an affectionate wife – and of good hopes in his profession. My second with a good deal of talent and in the way I trust of cultivating it to good purpose. Anne an honest downright good Scots lass in whom I would only wish to correct a spirit of satire – and Lockhart is Lockhart to whom I can most willingly confide the happiness [of the] daughter who chose him . . . . My dear wife, the partner of early cares and successes, is I fear frail in health. (*J.* 36, 7 Dec. 1825)

Then on 18 December:

> Ballantyne calld on me this morning. *Venit illa suprema dies.* My extremity is come. Cadell has received letters from London which all but positively announce the failure of Hurst and Robinson so that Constable and Coy must follow, and I must go with poor James Ballantyne for company. I suppose it will involve my all. . . . This news will make sad hearts at Darnick and in the cottages of Abbotsford which I do not nourish the least hope of preserving. It has been my Delilah and so I have often termed it – I was to have gone there on Saturday in joy and prosperity to receive my friends – my dogs will wait for me in vain – it is foolish – but the thoughts of parting from these dumb creatures have moved me more than any of the painful reflections I have put down . . . I must end this or I shall lose the tone of mind with which men should meet distress. I find my dogs' feet on my knees – I hear them whining and seeking me everywhere – this is nonsense but it is what they would do could they know how things are – poor Will Laidlaw – poor Tom Purdie – this will be news to wring your heart and many a poor fellow's besides to whom my prosperity was daily bread. . . . The feast of fancy is over with the feeling of independence. I can no longer have the delight of waking in the morning with bright ideas in my mind, haste to commit them to paper, and count them monthly as the means of planting such groves and purchasing such wastes . . . (*J.* 46–9)

From this point the journal is increasingly occupied with schemes of salvaging whatever can be saved from the wreck and with plans for work, cheered by the sympathy and generosity of friends. Almost every page at this stage records major or minor illness that stopped him working. After Christmas came the next blow, the decay of his wife's health. She died on 14 May. Scott had had to leave Abbotsford and go to Edinburgh to his duties in the law courts, but returned at once. Much has been made in biographies of Scott of the fact that his marriage was made on the rebound, a second-best affair. But Scott was not the man to live in happiness with any woman for thirty years and not be deeply affected by her loss.

> Lonely – aged – deprived of my family all but poor Anne – impoverished, an embarrassd man, I am deprived of the sharer of my thoughts and counsels who could always talk down my sense of calamitous apprehensions which break the heart that must bear them alone. . . . I wonder how I shall do with the large portion of thoughts which were hers for thirty years. I suspect they will be hers yet for a long time at least. (*J.* 167, 16 May 1826)

No man has portrayed the grief of bereavement better:

> I have been to her room: there was no voice in it – no stirring – the pressure of the coffin was visible on the bed but it had been removed elsewhere – All was neat as she loved it but all was calm – calm as death. I remembered the last sight of her – she raised herself in bed and tried to turn her eyes after me and said with a sort of smile 'You all have such melancholy faces.' They were the last words I ever heard her utter and I hurried away for she did not seem quite conscious of what she said – When I returnd immediately before departing she was in a deep sleep. It is deeper now. (*J.* 168, 18 May 1826)

He writes well of the strange dreamy feeling characteristic of such loss, which makes one feel like someone 'bewildered in a country where mist or snow has disguized those features of the landscape which are best known to him' and of the loneliness: 'the solitude seemd so absolute – my poor Charlotte would have been in the [room] half a score of times to see if the fire burnd and to ask a hundred kind questions' (*J.* 172, 26 May 1826). When he returned to his solitary lodgings in Edinburgh, it was worse: 'I am afraid poor Charles found me weeping – I do not know what other folks feel but with me the hysterical passion that compels tears is a terrible violence – a sort of throttling sensation – Then succeeded by a state of dreaming stupidity in which I ask if my poor Charlotte can actually be dead' (*J.* 174, 30 June 1826).

He turned to work as a distraction and ploughed on resolutely: 'my head aches – my eyes ache – my back aches – so does my breast – and I am sure my heart aches – And what can duty ask more?' (*J.* 177, 5 June 1826). He suffered all the petty ailments incidental to his situation: 'A dog howld all night and left me little sleep – poor cur! I dare say he had his distresses as I have mine' (*J.* 178, 8 June 1826). It takes a rare generosity or an unusual tenderness for dogs to react in this way to one that had deprived him of a night's rest, but it was also typical that in the next day's entry he should add, 'By the way how intolerably selfish this journal makes one seem. So much attention to one's naturals and non naturals' (*J.* 179, 9 June 1826). He was to stop the journal from July 1829 to May 1830 'because I thought it made me abominably selfish' (*J.* 663, 23 May 1830).

The journal is not all sad, nor does its author emerge as intolerably selfish. The man who could write one day 'Life could not be endured were it seen in [its] reality' (*J.* 53, 21 Dec. 1825) could also write:

> I generally affect good spirits in company of my family whether I am enjoying them or not. It is too severe to sadden the harmless mirth of others by suffering your own causeless melancholy to be seen. And this species of exertion is like virtue its own reward for the good spirits which are at first simulated become at length real. (*J.* 400–1, 24 Sept. 1827)

What is amazing is that, in the circumstances, so much of it is extremely cheerful, especially given the increasing ill health from which he suffered and the amount of work he was getting through. *Woodstock* had been finished shortly before the death of Lady Scott; the biography of Napoleon went churning on until June 1827. But in the meantime he had embarked on *Chronicles of the Canongate,* which contained the two brilliant stories 'The Highland Widow' and 'The Two Drovers'; 'The Surgeon's Daughter', however, was one of his more spectacular failures. In May 1827 he decided to write *Tales of a Grandfather*: a history of Scotland designed for the instruction and amusement of his little grandson, Johnnie Hugh Lockhart, inspired by J. W. Croker's *History of England* for children. But

> I will not write mine quite so simply as Croker has done. I am persuaded both children and the lower class of readers hate books which are written *down* to their capacity and love those that are more composed for their elders and betters. I will make if possible a book that a child will understand yet a man will feel some temptation to peruse. (*J.* 350, 24 May 1827)

The book ran eventually to four series and went through several editions in Scott's lifetime. In December 1827 he started *The Fair Maid of Perth*, which was published the following year, and almost immediately began on *Anne of Geierstein*. And from 1828 onwards he was continually occupied in revising the whole series of Waverley novels and the narrative poems for the Magnum edition, which was a joint money-spinning venture with Cadell to reduce the debt.

Time was running out. In January 1826 he had had what was probably a very slight stroke, from which he appeared to make a full recovery. In February 1830 he had a much more severe attack. It was from this point that Lockhart noticed an increasing cloudiness in Scott's prose. Further strokes followed in November 1830 and April 1831. The last was so severe that his life was despaired of, and all the family summoned. He insisted against medical advice on going on working, and *Castle Dangerous* was completed in September. But medical opinion insisted that he could not stand another winter in Scotland. Arrangements were made for a trip to Malta and Italy, and the Admiralty offered him and his party accommodation on one of its warships. They sailed on 29 October and reached Malta a month later, moving on to Naples, where Scott's son Charles was stationed, in December. In May 1832, they started for home by the land route, via Rome, Florence, Bologna, and Venice. In Nijmegen, he had a further cataclysmic stroke – 'the crowning blow', in Lockhart's words. After three weeks in London, he was transported back to Abbotsford, where he lingered, mainly in a state of semi-conscious delirium, until 21 September. He died, said Lockhart, on 'a beautiful day – so warm, that every window was wide open – and so perfectly still, that the sound of all others most delicious to his ear, the gentle ripple of the Tweed over its pebbles was distinctly audible as we knelt around the bed, and his eldest son kissed and closed his eyes'.[7]

7

Conclusion

So what, in the end, did it all amount to? With all the years of work and struggle, and the millions of words written, what did Scott accomplish for the novel? Coleridge summarized the achievement of Scott's work with his usual generosity:

> Scott's great merit, and at the same time, his *felicity*, and the true solution of the long-sustained *interest* novel after novel excites, lie in the nature of the subject, not merely, or even chiefly, because the struggle between the Stuarts and the Presbyterians and sectaries, is still in lively memory, and the passions of the adherency to the former, if not the adherency itself, extant in our own fathers' or grandfathers' times; nor yet (though this is of great weight) because the language, manners, etc., introduced are sufficiently different from our own for *poignancy*, and yet sufficiently near and similar for sympathy; nor yet because, for the same reason, the author, speaking, reflecting, and descanting in his own person, remains still (to adopt a painter's phrase) in sufficient *keeping* with his subject matter, while his characters can both talk and feel interesting to *us* as men, without recourse to *antiquarian* interest, and nevertheless without moral anachronism . . . – yet great as all these causes are, the essential wisdom and happiness of the subject consists in this, – that the contest between the loyalists and their opponents can never be *obsolete*, for it is the contest between the two great moving principles of social humanity; religious adherence to the past and the ancient, the desire and the admiration of permanence, on the one hand; and the passion for the increase of knowledge, for truth, as the offspring of reason – in short, the mighty instincts of *progression* and *free agency*, on the other. In all subjects of deep and lasting interest, you will detect a struggle between two opposites, two polar forces, both of which are alike necessary to our human well-being,

> and necessary each to the continued existence of the other. Well, therefore, may we contemplate with intense feelings those whirlwinds which are for free agents the appointed means, and the only possible condition of that equilibrium in which our moral Being subsists; while the disturbance of the same constitutes our sense of life.[1]

Carlyle, in his lengthy essay on Scott, which formed his review of Lockhart's *Life*, was less generous, though he makes some fair points. Scott, naturally, never read Carlyle's review, but coincidentally he answers many of the accusations in it in his dialogue with Captain Clutterbuck in the Introductory Epistle to *The Fortunes of Nigel*. 'Are you aware', asks the Captain, 'that an unworthy motive may be assigned for this rapid succession of publication? You will be supposed to work merely for the lucre of gain.' Scott replies:

> Supposing that I did permit the great advantages which must be derived from success in literature, to join with other motives in inducing me to come more frequently before the public, – that emolument is the voluntary tax which the public pays for a certain species of literary amusement – it is extorted from no one, and paid, I presume, by those only who can afford it, and who receive gratification in proportion to the expense. If the capital sum which these volumes have put into circulation be a very large one, has it contributed to my indulgences only? or can I not say to hundreds, from honest Duncan the paper manufacturer, to the most snivelling of printer's devils, 'Didst thou not share? Hadst thou not fifteen pence?' I profess I think our modern Athens much obliged to me for having established such an extensive manufacture.

And elsewhere, in equally defiant mood: 'No one shall find me rowing against the stream. I care not who knows it – I write for the public amusement.'

He defends himself against the accusation that he does not take time to arrange his story:

> I have repeatedly laid down my future work to scale, divided it into volumes and chapters, and endeavoured to construct a story which I meant should evolve itself gradually and strikingly, maintain suspense, and stimulate curiosity; and which, finally, should terminate in a striking catastrophe. But I think there is a daemon who seats himself on the feather of my pen when I begin to write, and leads it astray from the purpose. Characters expand

under my hand; incidents are multiplied; the story lingers, while the materials increase; my regular mansion turns out a Gothic anomaly, and the work is complete long before I have attained the point I proposed. . . . When I light on such a character as Bailie Jarvie, or Dalgetty, my imagination brightens, and my conception becomes clearer at every step which I make in his company, although it leads me many a weary mile away from the regular road, and forces me to leap hedge and ditch to get back into the route again.

This is Scott at his most characteristic, demistifying himself, justifying Carlyle's accusation that his only aim was to amuse:

> The Genius of rather a singular age – an age at once destitute of faith and terrified at scepticism . . . had said to himself: What man shall be the temporary comforter, or were it but the spiritual comfit-maker, of this my poor singular age, to solace its dead tedium and manifold sorrows a little? So had the Genius said, looking out over all the world, What man? and found him walking the dusty Outer Parliament-house of Edinburgh with his advocate-gown on his back; and exclaimed, That is he![2]

But Carlyle, who reckoned amusement low in the desiderata of human life even while he acknowledged that the amusement that the Waverley novels provided was of a high order (and who indexed fiction in one of his own books as 'idle, intolerable to the serious soul'), was not blind to one aspect of Scott's achievements:

> These Historical Novels have taught all men this truth, which looks like a truism, and yet was as good as unknown to writers of history and others, till so taught: that the bygone ages of the world were actually filled by living men, not by protocols, state-papers, controversies and abstractions of men. Not abstractions were they, not diagrams and theorems; but men, in buff or other coats and breeches, with colour in their cheeks, with passions in their stomach, and the idioms, features and vitalities of very men. It is a little work this; inclusive of great meaning! History will henceforth have to take thought of it. . . . It is a great service, fertile in consequences, this that Scott has done; a great truth laid open by him; – correspondent indeed to the substantial nature of the man; to his solidity and veracity even of imagination, which, with all his lively discursiveness, was the characteristic of him.[3]

Carlyle was right and history did thereafter take thought of it. In the words of G. M. Trevelyan, Scott 'not only invented the historical novel, but he enlarged the scope and revolutionized the study of history itself'; and he attributes this, not to Scott's overtly historical writing (like *The Life of Napoleon*) but to changes in the way people thought about the past, brought about by the work that started with *The Lay of the Last Minstrel* and continued through the series of Waverley novels; and this is in very truth due to what Carlyle had called Scott's veracity of imagination. He calls in evidence Macaulay, who, writing in the *Edinburgh Review* in 1828, said:

> Sir Walter Scott has used those fragments of truth which historians have scornfully thrown behind them, in a manner which may well excite their envy. He has constructed out of their gleanings works which, even considered as histories, are scarcely less valuable than theirs. But a truly great historian would reclaim those materials which the novelist has appropriated.[4]

It is a point also made by Heine, when he says that Scott's novels sometimes reproduce the spirit of English history much more faithfully than Hume. It is difficult, two centuries and many revolutions later, to think back into the historical attitudes and assumptions of eighteenth-century historians; but it has to be remembered, as Lukacs points out, that it was the French Revolution, the revolutionary wars, and the career of Napoleon that first made history a mass experience on a European scale. It was also these factors that stimulated feelings of patriotism and national pride that had not previously existed to anything like the same degree, and this too Lukacs ascribes to the consequences of the French Revolution:

> In its defensive struggle against the coalition of absolute monarchies, the French republic was compelled to create mass armies. The qualitative difference between mercenary and mass armies is precisely a question of their relations with the mass of the population. If in place of the recruitment or pressing into professional service of small contingents of the declassed, a mass army is to be created, then the content and purpose of the war must be made clear to the masses by means of propaganda. This happens not only in France itself during the defence of the Revolution and the later offensive wars. The other states, too, if they transfer to mass armies, are compelled to resort to the same means. . . . Such propaganda cannot possibly, however, restrict itself to the individual, isolated war. It has to reveal the social content, the historical

> presuppositions and circumstances of the struggle, to connect up the war with the entire life and possibilities of the nation's development.[5]

Scott was not only an antiquarian by nature; he spent his formative years in the upheavals that followed the French Revolution. He himself served in one of the volunteer regiments raised to defend the country against French invasion; his elder son, who entered the army professionally, was later an officer in a cavalry regiment. He understood instinctively the need to connect up the war with the entire life and possibilities of the nation's development, and not just the war that was taking place in his own lifetime, but the other major changes and upheavals that had taken place in his country in the previous two centuries. In all that he wrote, he saw the need for a reconciliation between the opposing forces, contest between whom ushered in any major change in constitution or monarch. He was not a reactionary: he understood, and in general supported, the need for change; but he understood equally the pain that change could inflict on the losing side, and frequently suffered it himself. His imagination was too generous to see the faults or virtues of one side only, wherever his own instinctive sympathies might lie, and his sympathies were not only romantic but also economic. He understood that the resentments that lay behind the Jacobite rebellions had little to do with whether a Stuart or a Hanoverian sat on the throne in London, but much to do with the fact that the Hanoverian settlement left the feudal chiefs unable to provide for their clansmen. He understood and sympathized with the Episcopalian side in the religious struggles of the seventeenth century (he had in fact become Episcopalian himself as soon as he was of an age to make his own choice), but he could equally sympathize with the principles that underlay the Calvinist faith in which he had been brought up, and nowhere does he treat the genuine followers of the Calvinist persuasion less than generously. His nondescript unexciting heroes are decent men, so placed that they can always see both sides of the question: it is indeed one of the main reasons for their mediocrity, that they are able to act as bridges between the two sides, seeing the virtues and vices of both. He looks back over history and he sees that the most bitter wars and disputes have eventually found a *via media* and have settled down in reconciliation, Saxon with Norman, Hanoverian with Jacobite, Whig with Tory, Puritan with Prelatist, and, most of all, Scotsman with Englishman.

For this reason it is inadequate to dismiss him as an escapist, most of all at the end of the twentieth century and the beginning of the twenty-first, when so much of the best of modern fiction is, like Scott's, being set in the past, and for not dissimilar reasons. Nor can anyone who influenced so much of the best of nineteenth-century European writing be lightly disregarded. His popularity in Europe during his lifetime was extraordinary. Goethe, who had started off by dismissing Scott with the words, 'I cannot learn anything from him. I have time only for the truly excellent,' was writing to Eckermann on 8 March 1831, 'Walter Scott is a great genius, who does not have an equal. . . . He gives me much to think about, and I discover in him a wholly new art, which has its own laws.'[6] Scott's novels were pirated in Germany often as soon as they were published in Edinburgh (sometimes, interestingly, under his own name, at a time when the author of *Waverley* was still hiding behind his anonymity at home). They were published in translation in the 1820s in France, Italy, and Hungary among other places. Manzoni was to write, *à propos* of his own *I Promessi Sposi,* 'se non ci fosse stato Walter Scott, a me non sarebbe venuto in mente di scrivere un romanzo'.[7] If it is considered that the novel as a literary form did not exist in Italy until Manzoni's *I Promessi Sposi,* it will be seen that Scott's influence on the development of Italian literature was even more incalculable.

He was directly to influence writers in Europe and America from Pushkin to Balzac and later. It is highly unlikely that Tolstoy's *War and Peace,* with its vivid battle scenes and its blend of historical and fictional characters, would have been written as it was if Scott had not written before him. Tolstoy said that he learned from Stendhal how to describe war; but Stendhal learned first from Scott to describe the confusion and revulsion that are experienced, for example, by Waverley and Henry Morton when they find themselves caught up on a battlefield and to understand the impact of history on those who are entangled in it. In *What is Art?* Tolstoy summarizes what he had in fact learned almost involuntarily from Scott about the art of the historical novel: 'What can be older than the relations of married couples, of parents to children, of children to parents; the relations of men to their fellow-countrymen, and to foreigners, to an invasion, to a defence, to property, to the land?'[8] If one adds to this his influence on Macaulay and the historians who followed him, it will be seen that what he produced was no mean body of work. His achievement was best summarized by his friend and political enemy Lord Cockburn, who had happened to be passing Abbotsford on the day of Scott's death, and noted in his journal, 'I saw [it] reposing beside its gentle Tweed, and amidst its fading woods, in the calm splendour of a sweet autumnal day. I was not aware till I reached Edinburgh that all that it then contained of him was his memory and his remains. Scotland never owed so much to one man.'[9]

Notes

CHAPTER 1. INTRODUCTION

1. Thomas Carlyle, *Critical and Miscellaneous Essays* (7 vols.; 1899), iv. 25.
2. F. A. Pottle, 'The Power of Memory in Boswell and Scott', in James Sutherland and F. P. Wilson (eds.), *Essays on the Eighteenth Century Presented to David Nichol Smith* (Oxford, 1945), 168.
3. Cadell to M. P. Stoniman, National Library of Scotland, MS 18110, fo.15.

CHAPTER 2. CHILDHOOD AND YOUTH

1. See Donald Sultana, *The Journey of Sir Walter Scott to Malta* (New York, 1986), and *The Siege of Malta Rediscovered* (Edinburgh, 1977).
2. Scott's future son-in-law, John Gibson Lockhart, matriculated at Glasgow University in 1805 at the age of 12.
3. John Sutherland, *The Life of Walter Scott* (Oxford, 1995), 28.

CHAPTER 3. THE POETRY

1. Thomas Percy, *Reliques of Ancient English Poetry*, ed. Henry B. Wheatley (3 vols.; New York, 1966), dedicatory epistle to the Countess of Northumberland, i. 1.
2. William Wordsworth, *Prose Works*, ed. W. J. B. Owen and S. W. Smyser (Oxford, 1974), iii. 78.
3. M. R. Dobie, 'The Development of Scott's *Minstrelsy*: an Attempt at a Reconstruction', *Transactions of the Edinburgh Bibliographical Society*, 2/1 (1946), 67–87.
4. John Sutherland, *The Life of Walter Scott* (Oxford, 1995), 86–7.

5. The extent to which Scott consciously or subconsciously plagiarized *Christabel* in *The Lay* was to be a subject of some dispute. See, e.g., Sutherland, *Life*, 100–2.
6. Sir Herbert Grierson, *Sir Walter Scott, Bart.: A New Life Supplementary to, and Corrective of, Lockhart's Biography* (1938), 101.
7. Sutherland, *Life*, 122–3.
8. *The Life and Correspondence of Robert Southey*, ed. R. C. Southey (6 vols.; 1850), iii. 140.
9. He did not get it. Even Constable took fright at this.
10. J. G. Lockhart, *Memoirs of the Life of Sir Walter Scott, Bart.* (5 vols.; 1837–8; repr. Adam and Charles Black, 1893), ch. XXXIV.

CHAPTER 4. THE EARLY NOVELS: *WAVERLEY* TO *THE ANTIQUARY*

1. J. G. Lockhart, *Memoirs of the Life of Sir Walter Scott, Bart.* (5 vols.; 1837–8; repr. Adam and Charles Black, 1893), ch. LXXXII.
2. John Sutherland, *The Life of Walter Scott* (Oxford, 1995), 167–70.
3. He was later to set down his views of them in his *Lives of the Novelists* (1820).
4. First published in *The Critical Review*, August 1794.
5. *Coleridge's Miscellaneous Criticism*, ed. T. M. Raysor (1936), 324.
6. Sutherland, *Life*, 190–1.

CHAPTER 5. THE LATER NOVELS

1. John Sutherland, *The Life of Walter Scott* (Oxford, 1995), 194.
2. Arnold Kettle, *An Introduction to the English Novel* (2 vols.; 1965), ii. 109.
3. Ibid. 112.
4. In this connection, however, see Jane Millgate, *Walter Scott: The Making of the Novelist* (London, 1984), 172.
5. Robert Irwin, 'Saladin and the Third Crusade: A Case Study in Historiography and the Historical Novel', in Michael Bentley (ed.), *Companion to Historiography* (1997), 39–52.

CHAPTER 6. CATASTROPHE AND *THE JOURNAL*

1. J. G. Lockhart, *Memoirs of the Life of Sir Walter Scott, Bart.* (5 vols.; 1837–8; repr. Adam and Charles Black, 1893), ch. LXIV.

2. Thomas Carlyle, *Critical and Miscellaneous Essays* (7 vols.; 1899), iv. 34.
3. Lockhart, *Memoirs*, ch. LXIV.
4. Ibid., ch. LXII.
5. Ibid., ch. LXIV.
6. John Sutherland, *The Life of Walter Scott* (Oxford, 1995), 289.
7. Lockhart, *Life*, ch. LXXXII.

CHAPTER 7. CONCLUSION

1. *Coleridge's Miscellaneous Criticism*, ed. T. M. Raysor (1936), 339–40.
2. Thomas Carlyle, *Critical and Miscellaneous Essays* (7 vols.; 1899), iv. 49–50.
3. Ibid. 77–8.
4. G. M. Trevelyan, in Allan Frazer (ed.), *Sir Walter Scott: An Edinburgh Keepsake* (Edinburgh, 1971), 27–8.
5. Georg Lukacs, *The Historical Novel*, trans. H. and S. Mitchell (1962), 23–4.
6. Quoted in Paul M. Ochojski, 'Waverley Ueber Alles', in Alan Bell (ed.), *Scott Bicentenary Essays* (Edinburgh, 1973), 264–5.
7. Quoted in R. D. S. Jack, 'Scott and Italy', in Bell (ed.), *Scott Bicentenary Essays*, 295.
8. Leo Tolstoy, *What is Art?*, ed. Gareth Jones, trans. Aylmer Maude (Bristol, 1994).
9. Henry Cockburn, *Journal, 1831–54* (2 vols.; Edinburgh, 1874), i. 37.

Glossary

abune, aboon above
afore before
ain own
amang among
ance once
ane one
anent about
anker a liquid or dry measure
aughty-nine eighty-nine
auld old
aye always, still
ayont beyond

bairn child
bide stay, remain
bield shelter
big, biggin' to build, building
blackcock black grouse
blithe, blither happy, happier
bonny pretty, handsome, good
brake bracken
braw fine, handsome
bred broad

carle man, fellow, labourer
carvy-seed carroway seed
cateran a Highland marauder
claymore broadsword
clout, clouted patch, patched

corbie carrion crow
cottar tenant or farmworker occupying a cottage
country district
creagh foray, raid
crowdie a mixture of oatmeal and water or a kind of curd cheese

dight attack, fight
dour hard, severe, obstinate

een, eyes
e'en even
eneugh enough

feifteen, the the Court of Session, consisting of fifteen judges
fold herd, pen
forpits a measure, a fourth part
frae from
friend relation

gae go
gang, ganging go, going
gar cause, make
gate way, direction
gauger exciseman
gear goods, possessions
gie give
gillies male servants or attendants
glower glare, scowl
gude good
guide direct, manage

hae, have
hame home
haylle strong
head behead
hearthstane hearthstone
hing, hinging hang, hanging

justify do justice upon, execute

kain rent paid in kind, often poultry
keepit kept
ken know

laird landowner, landlord
lang long
leddy lady
liferent a tenancy for the duration of life
linking active, energetic
loun common man
lug ear

mailing a tenant farm or piece of land
mair more
maist most
maun must
mony many
muckle much
muir moor

ones once
ony any
oursells ourselves
owerlay a folded collar or cravat; a piece of material folded back on itself

part, parting divide, being divided
peeble throw pebbles at
peysse, peace
puir poor
pund pound

recks matters
reise branch, twig, stick
reiver robber, raider
rickle something dilapidated or loosely thrown together, broken down
rive, riven tear up, destroy; destroyed
rub, rubbit rob, robbed

sae so

sark shirt
sey cut of beef from shoulder to loin
shealings place where winnowing was done
sib related to
sic, siclike such
siller silver, money
sorning scrounging, begging importunately
sough a deep sigh, sound of wind or water
sporran pouch worn in front of the kilt
spreagherie booty, plunder
stanes stones
stirk young bullock
stounde time
suld should
sunket sweetmeat, delicacy

tae to, too, toe
taen taken
tack lease, tenancy
thack thatch
thegither together
thigging begging, cadging
thrapple throat
tirrivy fit of rage, tantrum
tod fox
twa, two

unco strange, unfamiliar, extraordinary

waefu' woeful
wark work
weans children
weel well
whilk which
whisht hush
wife woman
winna will not
wot know
wynne joy, pleasure

yestreen last night

Select Bibliography

(The place of publication is London, unless otherwise specified.)

WORKS BY SIR WALTER SCOTT

Editions

Novels

There are innumerable editions of Scott's work, particularly of the novels. The first complete edition, published for the most part under Scott's supervision and with his notes, is the Magnum edition (1829–33). For consistency, all references in the text to novels are to this edition; all references are to the chapter.

The standard text of the novels in the future is likely to be the Edinburgh University edition under the general editorship of David Hewitt, which is currently being produced, but this edition aims to return to the first edition of each novel, printing the introduction and notes supplied by Scott for the Magnum edition in separate volumes at the end of the series. Readers who desire or need to have the supplementary introductions and notes at hand while reading the novel will find this inconvenient, and should turn to the many good editions published by the World's Classics, Everyman, and Penguin. Many of the newer editions contain interesting critical introductions. The short stories were edited by Lord David Cecil in the World's Classics (1934).

Poems

There are numerous editions of the poems, both of individual poems and of collections, the first in eleven volumes by his son-in-law, John Gibson Lockhart (1833–4). The poetical works were edited by J. L. Robinson in the Oxford Standard Authors series (1904). A convenient paperback selection is *Selected Poems*, ed. James Reed, published in the Fyfield Books series by Carcanet Press (Manchester, 1992). Some recently discovered poems were edited by Davidson Cook in *New Love Poems* (Oxford, 1932). See also William Ruff, 'A Bibliography of the Poetical Works of Sir Walter Scott, 1796–1832', *Transactions of the Edinburgh Bibliographical Society* (1936–7), 99–239.

Journal

The best edition of Scott's *Journal* is that edited by W. E. K. Anderson (Oxford, 1972; paperback edition, Canongate Classics, Edinburgh, 1998).

Letters and papers

The only edition of Scott's letters remains the 12-volume edition of Sir Herbert Grierson (1932), which should be read in conjunction with James Corson, *Notes and Index to Sir Herbert Grierson's Edition of The Letters of Sir Walter Scott* (Oxford, 1979). The first volume of Sir Herbert's edition contains a full statement by James Glen, WS, of Scott's financial transactions, which is indispensable reading for anyone hoping to unravel this subject. For letters to Scott, see W. Partington (ed.), *The Private Letter-Books of Sir Walter Scott* (1930) and *Sir Walter's Post Bag* (1932).

The Abbotsford Collection of Scott's letters and papers and those of his immediate family is held in the National Library of Scotland.

Essays and reviews

A selection of Scott's literary essays and reviews is published in *Sir Walter Scott on Novelists and Fiction*, ed. Ioan Williams (1968).

Selected Works

The Minstrelsy of the Scottish Border (1802–3).
The Lay of the Last Minstrel (1805).
Marmion (1808).
Life and Works of John Dryden (1808).
The Lady of the Lake (1810).
Rokeby (1813).
The Bridal of Triermain (1813).
Waverley (1814).
Guy Mannering (1814).
Life and Works of Jonathan Swift (1814).
The Lord of the Isles (1815).
The Antiquary (1816).
The Black Dwarf (1816).
Old Mortality (1816).
Rob Roy (1817).
The Heart of Midlothian (1818).
The Bride of Lammermoor (1819).
A Legend of Montrose (1819).
Ivanhoe (1819).
The Monastery (1820).
The Abbot (1820).
Kenilworth (1821).
The Pirate (1821).
Peveril of the Peak (1822).
The Fortunes of Nigel (1822).
Quentin Durward (1823).
Redgauntlet (1824).
St Ronan's Well (1824).
The Betrothed (1825).
The Talisman (1825).
Lives of the Novelists (1825).
Woodstock (1826).
The Life of Napoleon (1827).
'The Highland Widow' (1827).
'The Two Drovers' (1827).
'The Surgeon's Daughter' (1827).
The Fair Maid of Perth (1828).
Anne of Geierstein (1829).
Castle Dangerous (1831).
Count Robert of Paris (1831).

BIBLIOGRAPHY

Corson, James, *A Bibliography of Sir Walter Scott* (Edinburgh, 1943). The standard reference work.

Rubinstein, Jill, *Sir Walter Scott: A Reference Guide* (Boston, 1978). For later material.

The MLA annual bibliography should be consulted for work post-1977.

BIOGRAPHY

Scott on Himself, ed. David Hewitt (Scottish Academic Press, 1981). Scott wrote a memoir of his own early life, known as the Ashiesteil Fragment (1808), which was incorporated by his son-in-law, Lockhart, in his life (see below). It is edited here, along with other autobiographical fragments of writing.

There are innumerable biographies by other hands, of which the most important are:

Buchan, John, *Sir Walter Scott* (1932). Biographically, little advance on Lockhart, but some interesting critical perspectives from a Scottish novelist who was a successor to and admirer of Scott.

Chambers, R., *Life of Sir Walter Scott* (1834; rev. 1871).

Corson, J. C. (ed.), *Sir Walter Scott in Italy: Sir William Gell's Reminiscences* (1957). Lockhart included a large part of this document in his biography. It covers the months of his stay in Naples in 1832, when Scott's mind was clouded and largely destroyed by the strokes he had suffered.

Daiches, David, *Sir Walter Scott and his World* (1971).

Grierson, Sir Herbert, *Sir Walter Scott, Bart. A New Life Supplementary to, and Corrective of, Lockhart's Biography* (1938). Grierson (who had a fine understanding of Scott as a writer) was the first critic to point out discrepancies and manipulations of date in Lockhart's work, and he also devoted much attention to the tangled question of Scott's finances and bankruptcy, to elucidate which, he had the help of a professional accountant (see under Letters above). Essential reading. It can profitably be read together with Grierson's lecture, 'Lang, Lockhart and Biography' in Grierson, *Essays and Addresses* (1940) (see under Criticism and Background Studies below).

Hogg, James, *Domestic Manners and Private Life of Sir Walter Scott* (Glasgow, 1834). Hogg's memoir of the private moments of the Scott family caused Scott's children great offence when it was published, but the book is not without interest. There is a modern edition by Douglas Mack, *James Hogg's Anecdotes of Sir Walter Scott* (Edinburgh, 1983).

Johnson, Edgar, *Sir Walter Scott, The Great Unknown* (2 vols.; 1970). An exhaustive and largely sympathetic account, mostly biographical, but with separate chapters of criticism on the works. The most irritating feature of the book is the arrangement of the notes, which makes consulting them an unnecessarily complicated process.

Johnston, C. N. (Lord Sands), *Sir Walter Scott's Congé* (1929). An account of Scott's unsuccessful courtship of Williamina Belsches, which is of some significance in the study of his work. The revised third edition (1931) tackled and solved some chronological problems in Lockhart's *Life*.

Lang, Andrew, *Sir Walter Scott* (1896).

Lockhart, J. G., *Memoirs of the Life of Sir Walter Scott, Bart.* (5 vols.; 1837–8; repr. Adam and Charles Black, 1893). Lockhart's biography is the essential starting point for any Scott studies, although it has been shown in recent years that his treatment of letters and dates is often unreliable. It is none the less an unparalleled portrait of a man whom he knew and loved better than most people. The many later biographies that are merely recensions or abbreviations of Lockhart are not listed here.

Pearson, Hesketh, *Walter Scott: His Life and Personality* (1954).

Pope-Hennessy, Una, *Sir Walter Scott* (1948). Divided into two sections, the life and the work. Maintains that several of the later novels were actually written before *Waverley*.

Quayle, Eric, *The Ruin of Sir Walter Scott* (1968). Quayle, a descendant of the Ballantyne brothers, resents the treatment of them in Lockhart's biography (which was unjust) and his book is largely a demolition job both of Scott and of Lockhart.

Speaight, Robert, 'Scott and the Biographers', *Ariel*, 2/3 (1971).

Sutherland, John, *The Life of Walter Scott* (Oxford, 1995). A much more critical version than Johnson's, but with some interesting perspectives on both the life and the work. Sutherland is particularly interesting in setting Scott's achievements in the context of the history of publishing and the book trade.

Wood, G. A. M., 'The Great Reviser; or the Unknown Scott', *Ariel*, 2/3 (1971).

CRITICISM AND BACKGROUND STUDIES

[Adolphus, J. L.], *Letters to Richard Heber, Esq. Containing critical remarks on the series of novels beginning with 'Waverley', and an attempt to ascertain their author* ([1821]). An extremely acute and interesting demonstration that the *Waverley* novels were by the same hand as *The Lay of the Last Minstrel*, *Marmion*, and the other poems.

Alexander, J. H., and Hewitt, David (eds.), *Scott and his Influence* (Edinburgh, 1983).

Batho, Edith C., *The Ettrick Shepherd: James Hogg* (Cambridge, 1927).

Bell, Alan (ed.), *Scott: Bicentenary Essays* (Edinburgh, 1973). See particularly the essays by Edgar Johnson and David Daiches.

Buchan, David, *The Ballad and the Folk* (1972).

Carlyle, Thomas, *Critical and Miscellaneous Essays* (7 vols.; 1889). This should be read in conjunction with Sir Herbert Grierson's lecture, 'Scott and Carlyle', in Grierson, *Essays and Addresses* (1940) (see below).

Clark, A. M., *Sir Walter Scott: The Formative Years* (New York, 1970).

Cockshut, A. O. J., *The Achievement of Sir Walter Scott* (1969).

Constable, Thomas, *Archibald Constable and his Literary Correspondents* (3 vols.; Edinburgh, 1873).

Craig, David, *Scottish Literature and the Scottish People, 1680–1830* (1961).

Crawford, T. C., *Scott* (Edinburgh, 1965).

Daiches, David, 'Scott's Achievement as a Novelist', in *Literary Essays* (Edinburgh and London, 1966).

Davie, Donald, *The Heyday of Sir Walter Scott* (1961).

Devlin, D. D., *The Author of Waverley* (1971).

Dobie, M. R., 'The Development of Scott's *Minstrelsy*: An Attempt at a Reconstruction', *Transactions of the Edinburgh Bibliographical Society*, 2/1 (1946). Indispensable for students of the ballads.

Duncan, Ian, *Modern Romance and Transformations of the Novel* (Cambridge, 1992).

Frazer, Allan (ed.), *Sir Walter Scott: An Edinburgh Keepsake* (Edinburgh, 1971). A selection of the addresses delivered at the annual dinners of the Walter Scott Club between 1927 and 1971. They are uneven in quality and some have dated, but the best of them (e.g. Sir Herbert Grierson, G. M. Trevelyan, C. S. Lewis, and David Daiches) are still well worth reading.

Gaston, Patricia, *The Waverley Prefaces: A Reading of Sir Walter Scott's Prefaces to the Waverley Novels* (New York, 1991).

Grierson, Sir Herbert, *Essays and Addresses* (1940).

Hart, Francis R., *Scott's Novels: The Plotting of Historical Survival* (Virginia, 1966).

[Hazlitt, William], *The Spirit of the Age: Or Contemporary Portraits* (1825). Much of Hazlitt's criticism of Scott was coloured by their differences in politics and his hostility to Scott's Toryism, but this is a fine critical essay.

Irwin, Robert, 'Saladin and the Third Crusade: A Case Study in Historiography and the Historical Novel', in M. Bentley (ed.), *Companion to Historiography* (1997).

Jeffrey, Francis, *Contributions to the Edinburgh Review* (4 vols.; 1844). Contains some of Jeffrey's original reviews of the Waverley novels.

Kettle, Arnold, *An Introduction to the English Novel* (2 vols.; 1965). A Marxist view of the subject but with a very good chapter on *The Heart of Midlothian*.

Lang, Andrew, *Sir Walter Scott and the Border Minstrelsy* (1910).

Lascelles, Mary, *The Storyteller Retrieves the Past* (Oxford, 1980).

Lukacs, Georg, *The Historical Novel*, trans. H. and S. Mitchell (1962).

MacQueen, John, *The Enlightenment and Scottish Literature* (Edinburgh, 1989). Useful background to Scott's literary formation.

McMaster, Graham, *Scott and Society* (Cambridge, 1981).

Mayo, R. D., 'The Chronology of the Waverley Novels: The Evidence of the Manuscripts', *Publications of the Modern Language Association of America*, 63 (Sept. 1948). An answer to Una Pope-Hennessy's arguments (see under Biography above) on the order in which the novels were written.

Millgate, Jane, *Walter Scott: The Making of the Novelist* (1984).

—— *Scott's Last Edition* (Edinburgh, 1987).

Muir, Edwin, *Scott and Scotland: The Predicament of the Scottish Writer* (1936). Very much a meditation on the state of Scottish literature since the Union of the Parliaments in 1707 and Scott's place in the literary tradition. See also his essays on Scott in Muir, *Essays on Literature and Society* (1949) and in W. L. Renwick (ed.), *Sir Walter Scott Lectures 1940–48* (see below).

Oliver, John, 'Scottish Poetry in the Earlier Nineteenth Century', in James Kinsley (ed.), *Scottish Poetry: A Critical Survey* (1955).

Oman, Carola, *The Wizard of the North* (1973).

Parsons, C. O., *Witchcraft and Demonology in Scott's Fiction* (Edinburgh, 1964).

Pottle, F. A., 'The Power of Memory in Boswell and Scott', in James Sutherland and F. P. Wilson (eds.), *Essays on the Eighteenth Century Presented to David Nichol Smith* (Oxford, 1945). An invaluable essay, particularly interesting on the function of memory in neo-classic and Romantic periods.

Renwick, W. L. (ed.), *Sir Walter Scott Lectures 1940–48* (1950). Lectures by Sir Herbert Grierson, Edwin Muir, G. M. Young, and S. C. Roberts, reprinted from the *Edinburgh University Journal* (where the lectures for 1950–6 can be found).

Sultana, Donald, *The Siege of Malta Rediscovered* (Edinburgh, 1977).

—— *The Journey of Sir Walter Scott to Malta* (New York, 1986).

Whibley, Charles (ed.), *Collected Essays of W. P. Ker* (2 vols.; 1925). Vol. i contains three essays on Scott.

Wilson, A. N., *The Laird of Abbotsford* (Oxford, 1980).

Wittig, Kurt, *The Scottish Tradition in Literature* (Edinburgh and London, 1958).

Index